THE LOSS OF HUMANITY

CLAVER LUKOKI

ISBN: **9798654196552**

Published by Author Prime.

Printed in the United Kingdom.

THE LOSS OF HUMANITY

Claver Lukoki

PLEASE NOTE: All Bible references are gotten from the **KING JAMES VERSION, NEW INTERNATIONAL VERSION, NEW LIVING TRANSLATION, AND AMPLIFIED VERSION** of the Bible except where otherwise stated.

TABLE OF CONTENTS

ENDORSEMENT

The compelling fact of Claver Lukoki's life is that he carries a burning passion to impact, envision and influence his generation to rise to their God intended purpose and to make a difference in their own lives and their generation. His book contains great revelation knowledge. If you are not sure of your life's worth and purpose, I highly recommend this book to you.

Bishop Abel Kungu Snr. President & Apostolic leader of Acts of Faith Ministries international & Acts of faith ministerial association (AFMA) Bedford, United Kingdom.

WORDS FROM
THE NEXT GENERATION

The Next Generation is a group of young kids that I help and mentor in understanding of their original purpose that is confined to the vision of their lives. Here are some of their testimonies under my mentorship program.

Purpose was something I thought was an achievement you learn further down the line in life as you grow up. But I've learnt that it can start right now and can only be done with God's help. Moreover, I've learnt that planning what I want to do further on in life is difficult in a world of 24/7 access to information .So getting a head start with Claver has been hugely beneficial and I'm learning more about myself as well every day.

- Janeil Banghar

I used to think that you had to be an adult to discover your purpose but now I know it can be done at any age with the help of the Lord. This is only the start and Claver has helped me with it. To be honest I would've never thought of doing this but I'm lucky to have Claver. This is only the beginning.   -Abel kunguJnr

I always thought that purpose was for adults and I'm just a kid, so I'm not supposed think about any of that. Now Claver has taught me that it is best to know your purpose when you are young and to have a plan so you know what to do in life. Your life revolves around your purpose and plan and if you don't know your purpose or have plan then what is the purpose of your life? If you were building a house would you do it without a plan? If not then why are you living your life without a plan. "A goal without a plan is just a dream" - Antoine de Saint-Exupéry. When I am older (or even now) I aspire to be an Actress but I can't do that without a plan. This is not an easy job to get into but I need to work hard. I am so blessed to have Claver in my life because without him I would not have discovered my purpose or had this opportunity so thank you. This is just the beginning of my life.

- Tiaara Mpanumpanu

Purpose is something I had but didn't see. Something I longed for but didn't allow. I overlooked my purpose in a battle to figure out who I was & who I wanted to be. In a world with millions of people it would be silly to think you have to get through life alone without guidance or support from your loved ones. Asking for help can be hard, I've been there, however being surrounded by people who are willing to help out of the kindness of their own heart is rare. Claver not only took his time to help me understand the purpose of my existence but many others alongside me. I was already on my journey figuring out my purpose and was blessed with help along the way. I was a dreamer with no plans I was filled with just hopes and dreams with no blueprint to follow. Step by step I began to understand the importance of a plan to reach my goals and live up to the expectations I had placed on myself. Writing a plan is easy following it and being motivated to achieve each step without skipping ones in-between not so much but day by day I continue to work on it. Patience is something I lack I cannot lie but all good things take time. Life consists of battles we are unaware of ones that could easily throw you off track I would be lying if I said having a plan to look back on isn't helpful in those unexpected times. God has a plan for me and with his guidance and the guidance of many more my purpose remains an open door...   – Anesu Tapfumaneyi

ACKNOWLEDGEMENTS

First and foremost, I would like to thank my Lord Jesus Christ. In the process of putting this book together, I realised how privileged I am and how I have been favoured enough to write this book. Through the Holy Spirit, I have been enabled to have deeper insights and revelations of the word and a knowing of my purpose. None of this would have been accomplished without my Father God. Therefore, I thank you Lord God for giving me the power to believe in my passion and pursue my purpose and dreams. Without the Grace and the mercy of the Lord, I would not have been able to finalise this book.

To my Father and Mother, Kiyedi Lukombo and Kimbinga Mpembele Lukombo: I am truly blessed to call you my parents. I have come to the realisation that words are not enough to express my gratitude for all the wisdom, love and support you've given me. You are and have always been my number one fan and for that, I am eternally grateful. I pray that I will be a good parent to my children as you were and have always been to me.

To my brothers and sisters, I just want to say that I deeply love you all from the deepest depths of my heart. You all have always made me feel appreciated and loved at all times. I am amazed by your support always and I pray that this book will also help you to discover your ultimate purpose in Christ and live it out for the glory of God in Jesus Christ our Lord.

To my little brother Bradley and Nephew Omari: my only prayer for you both is that as you two grow older, that you will come into the knowledge of Christ Jesus and pursue him alone for the rest of your life, that you two will know and fulfil your purpose to the LORD your God. Obey his directions, laws, commands, rules, and written instructions as they are recorded in His word. Then you'll succeed in everything you do wherever you guys may go. I love you guys always.

My sincere thanks to my pastors, Bishop Abel, Success Kungu, Pastor Freddy, Lillian Maleka and Pastor Zorka Crichlow: I just want to say I am forever grateful and thankful for your continuous patience, love and prayers. You all have given your lives to serve and support individuals like myself, thank you for believing in me and for the gift that has been bestowed upon by the Lord to glorify Him.

I thank the Next Generation Youths, thank you for all your support and encouragement. You are the best and you have all motivated me to grow in my walk with the Lord and to become a better a leader. I pray that this book will also empower you to walk in your purpose.

To my fiancé, Rita Ndozi: Thank you very much for your love and constant support, you are the most amazing, wonderful and beautiful woman I have ever met. You have no Idea how happy you make me. Everyday day with you feels like a dream but I know it is a reality and I'm so blessed and thankful to the almighty God to have you in my life. There is nobody else I rather have to fulfil my purpose with but you alone. Thank you for loving me, and thank you for making me feel so loved. I love you more than words can say. God knows. Thank you.

Finally, a big thank you to all my other family and friends. Although, I did not precise mention your names, all your support and encouragement is invaluable.

FOREWORD

Having no clue how but believing that I could publish my book within a month, I decided it was now time to begin to build connections with local publishers. With some doubts, I wondered whether my decision was worth pursuing. No author owed me a dime yet alone offer me their time to give me an insight to self-publishing.

After a year of procrastination and agonising research that lead to self inflicted pressure to release my book within a month's deadline. I began to panic grasping every bit of faith I had left that God was going to make a way. Then there came an olive branch. Peace from the turmoil. I happened to stumble upon Claver Lukoki's Instagram page. The bible says in the last days, the love of many will grow cold. But apart from many there are the likes of Claver a true brother, who without the expectation of gain extended a helping hand to clarify the answers I needed to finalise the publication of my very first book.

I look up to him knowing he had become a publisher before myself having written the book 'The Purpose of Existence' that blessed me. I never thought as I flooded him with all the questions I had, that one day I would receive the honour to have my words included in his charge. With joy, I am more than happy to present to you the writings of a man who's kindness has proven to resemble the love of Christ Jesus.

I believe that this book was written with no malice agenda, but to enlighten you with the truth that the Lord has bestowed upon Claver's heart and mind. This truth will bring about understanding of your purpose on earth and our God who created it. I encourage you to open your heart to receive every word that will enliven and in-line you with purpose beyond the ordinary.

By Benie Nkosi

The author of "You've Still Got It" Book.

INTRODUCTION

F irst and foremost, get this! Whatever you don't ADMIRE you can't DESIRE, whatever you don't DESIRE you can't DISCOVER and whatever you don't DISCOVER you can't ACQUIRE. Admire says "I love it", desire says "I want it", discover says "I know it" while acquire says "I have it". Thus, this book triggers your love (admiration). for the pursuit (desire) of purpose and gives you a visual knowledge (discovery) in achieving (acquisition) what you were originally created for. Therefore, this book aims to give you a deeper understanding of yourself; and of course, you should know that life is not worth living when it's not in accordance to its purpose.

More so, may I dislodge this truth to your sentiment; one of the greatest tragedies of humanity is not death but to "exist" and not "live", the former talks about dormancy and unfruitfulness, while the latter emphasizes impact and productivity. A life that exists, has just occupied a space in the earth but a life that fulfils the reason for its existence, is said to make an impact to the earth. Until you work on your purpose for existence, you have just been existing and not living. Hence, this book stretches your desire and thirst in bridging your discovery of purposes into actualising them. It is about you discovering the reason for your being and the reason as to why you are here on planet earth.

Finally, it is about you understanding that there is more to life than most of you think and as a result, this book aims directly to usher you into your destiny, to live like there is no tomorrow. To serve as a reminder that you were not born just to pay bills, work and die, but rather to live a significantly fulfilled life. This book is not just a literature but a message to unleash and ignite the reality of your life via illuminating your mind to the efficacies of a purposeful living Therefore, join me on this journey of self-discovery and walk into your destiny

PREFACE

The search and yearning for the understanding and knowledge of the purpose of our existence has confused humanity for thousands of years. Mankind is yet to fully accept where we have originated from, why we are here on earth, what we are born to do. Additionally, the longing for knowledge about our existence has led us to seek understanding from wrong sources. As a result, it has caused pain and agony in our yearning hearts, hoping that if we live our lives as we want then maybe one day this hunger will come to an end. However, it just seems as if this craving in our hearts will never stop until we get answers to the "why" are we here on this earth question. Thus, for centuries we have been trying to look into ourselves to come up with some form of

14

explanation of what human beings are made of and where we originated.

In the process of that, we have created our own theories as humans; one concept is that of the "evolution" in the hope that it will fulfil our yearning hearts and heal the bruise of the depths of our heart from the questions that we have in our minds concerning our existence. But creating our own theories will never reveal our life's purpose. In the manuscript of God (the Bible) it says, "It is God who directs the lives of His creatures; everyone's life is in His power."[1]This is contrary to what many popular books, movies and seminars tell us. However, please note that you will never discover your life's worth or meaning just by consulting yourself. That is because you didn't create yourself, so there is no way you can tell yourself what you were created for and what you are made of. If I hand you an invention that you have never seen before you wouldn't know its purpose, and the invention itself wouldn't be able to tell you either, only the creator or the owner's manual could reveal its purpose. Therefore, the answers to our yearning

---

[1]Job 12:10, In his hand is the life of every creature and the breath of all mankind.

heart will never be revealed or answered by another human being.

God has not left us in the dark to wonder and guess. He has clearly revealed His purposes for our existence through the Bible. It is our Owner's manual, explaining why we are alive, how life works, what to avoid, and what to expect in the future. It describes what no self-help or philosophical books are capable of explaining. The Bible says, "God's wisdom is something mysterious that goes deep into the interior of his purposes. You don't find it lying around on the surface. It's not the latest message, but more likely, the oldest - what God determined as the way to bring out his best in us, long before we ever arrived on the scene." 1 Corinthians 2:7. (MSG).

Pastor Rick states the following "God is not just the starting point of your life; He is the Source of it".[i]To discover your purpose of existence in this life you must turn to God's word, not the world's wisdom. You must build your life on eternal truths, not psychology, success motivation, or inspirational stories. The Bible says, "It's in Christ that we find out who we are and what we are living for. Long before we first heard of Christ and got our hopes up, he had his eyes on us, had designs on us for glorious living, part of the overall purpose he is working out in everything and everyone." Ephesians 1:11, 12. (MSG).

I remember growing up, as a young man; I was desperately searching and yearning to know the purpose of my existence on this planet. Large bunch of people I spent most of my time with would abuse me emotionally on a daily basis. I was regularly called degrading names; I remember someone once said to me that " it was better your mother gave birth to a dog instead of you". Life became unbearable for me at one point; I was living in so much pain, so much hurt in my heart. Until one day, I was introduced to Jesus Christ and He began to answer my question. Life started to make a lot more sense, and as I continue on this journey with God, I can now see and live my life with purpose.

As a living testimony of what faith and seeking God can do, I truly believe that as you navigate through this book, you will surely discover the purpose you were created for and where you came from, that you will begin to live your life effectively on this planet earth as the Creator intended for your life. The purpose of your life fits into a much larger purpose that God has designed for eternity. That's exactly what this book is about; you discovering your purpose and living it out loud.

LIFE OF PURPOSE

I honestly believe that if we are willing to live a fulfilled life on this planet earth we must, we shall and we have to let go of all the strong holds that is bringing each of us down spiritually and physically, if we must fulfil our purposes in life. A fulfilled life is a life that has been long subjected to the path of purpose. Little wonders why there is a huge difference between being rich and being fulfilled, another obvious difference between making money and achieving purpose.

The world, in the latest century has incorporated some outright dissenting and vague views of what success or achieving purpose really mean. Achieving purpose in life has been confused to:

1. Making Money or being rich

A lot of people, due to the economic imbalance and pursuit to escape abject poverty, have seen money as a purpose that must be achieved. Therefore, when their struggles attract favour and tremendously change in a particular season and they advance in income or financial worth, they conclude that they are successful or they assume they have achieved purpose. Many times purpose has been reduced to money, which is highly far from it. Man is too loaded on the inside and God is too wise to create us for the purpose of making money. Sadly, when many people are asked to mention or highlight the successful men in the world, they go about giving a list of rich men. Of course, making money surfaces alongside, fulfilling of purpose. Nevertheless, of a truth, hardly have I seen a successful man who is poor! I know questions might pop up in your mind saying, what then is the difference, how then do we identify the rich man from the successful man? Good!

There is a salient and vivid difference. A Man can be rich without being successful, Successful in the sense of purpose achievement. Get this; a man is successful when he has duly and fully achieved purpose. The gauge for success is not in money making but in actualising your potentials to the maximum and making impact in the lives of others. In other words, money was never and will not be a parameter to scale your level of success but your God's given purpose. Although, a man of purpose attracts money and sees himself being affluent not because money was his goal but because it is natural for money to be attracted to a problem solver, it is natural for riches to be glued to someone who is impacting lives tremendously.

Wherever there is "VIRTUE" you will see "VALUE". Invariably, how "WELL" you have built your talents, gifts and potentials determines how much of "VALUE" you receive. The value can either come in money or other commensurate resources. Take for instance, the price of a land with no structure on it will be different from the price of a land with structure on it. What makes the difference? Both of them discovered the same resources but one has improved on his land; that is, built a structure on it, while the other left his land plain and natural.

2. Fame

Furthermore, fame is another element this present age has confused for success. Being famous is not a measure for identifying someone who has lived a fulfilled (purposeful) life. That a man is widely known doesn't mean he has fulfilled destiny. Methuselah, as recorded in the bible happens to be the oldest man on earth, which makes him widely known. The bone of contention is, how many things can you highlight about him as a trend, path or life lessons you can inculcate? Virtually none, right? Does it now occur to you that popularity is not the primary gauge for fulfilment? Although, popularity comes by and with achieving purpose but it's not the principal focus. Why then should we use purpose and fame interchangeably in expressing the extent of success?

God has made every man's purpose uniquely. Additionally, anyone who achieves purpose has a very high tendency of being famous for what he's doing because the purpose of a man announces him.

One more thing several others confuse for purpose is positional leadership. You here words like; At last, he achieved his purpose of becoming the president. Finally, he has reached the peak of success by being appointed as the minister of health. Alas! The contract he won made him the most fulfilled and successful in his family, because the money runs in millions of dollars. Positional leadership is far from it, when it comes to purpose. Besides, a position can't be a man's purpose; instead, it could be a means to achieving the purpose. Hence, success in leadership is not how many YEARS you use in office but how many LIVES you touch with the office. Positional leadership isn't a basic criterion for success but could act as a catalyst to enhance it.

Take for instance, while King Saul still ruled as king over Israel, the spirit of the lord already left him and David was hereby anointed as a king, according to 1Samuel16:1 *"And the Lord said unto Samuel, how long will thou mourn for Saul, seeing that, I have rejected him from being king over Israel? Fill thine oil and go, I will send thee to the house of Jesse the Bethlehemite: for I have provided me a king among his sons"* **(KJV)**

What I have seen in leadership is this; when God anoints you, men will appoint you. For

David to face Goliath, he had-not just a skill or experiences- the anointing of leadership in him. Some of the characteristics of good leadership are courage and prudence. When David conquered and killed Goliath, his "purpose" in the land of Israel became glaring and conspicuous. Thereafter, the bible says women began to sing his praise and that was a show of "positional leadership", they wanted him to be king over them. When a man fulfils purpose, he will always be the people's choice because he has something to offer. You don't need to be the HEAD to be AHEAD, but being AHEAD makes men put you as their HEAD. Get this! It's something for someone to be a "LEADER" and it's another thing for someone to be in "CHARGE". During the defeat of Goliath, Saul was the king (leader) but David was in charge. Anyone who helps in meeting the need at a certain time is the one in charge for that space of time.

In relation to the expositions of right ideologies about purpose given above, we can say money, fame and positional leadership are shadows, while the real image we ought to seek after is purpose.

Series of men, who have trended on this path of purpose through achieving destiny, they got it by a conscious effort of discovering what is meant for them and what is not meant for them. Therefore, it is highly expedient that a man who must fulfil purpose must shed off every weight that could serve as barrier to his greater height. Of course, there are weights that easily beset man.

What exactly do I refer to as Weights?

1. Poisonous Pleasure

They are things that look pleasurable to you but highly detrimental to fulfilling your destiny. Just like Delilah was good at the sight of Samson and seem pleasurable to him, the same Delilah was the love of Samson yet she was the danger Samson needed to run from. As per Samson, Delilah was the weight he needed to let go. Samson loved Delilah so much that even when he forgot and declined the instructions given to him not marry from a strange land. Many times it is always hard for people to shed off their weight because they are so much engrossed in it.

2. They could be Evil Company (ungodly friends)

The scriptures say "evil communications corrupt good manners". When a man is surrounded by friends who are ungodly there are higher tendencies that the bad influence will thwart his path to fulfilling his purpose. One of the present day determinants of where someone is heading to or will end his life is by checking his team of friends. A well-known general saying; "show me your friend and I will tell you who you are" has over time proved to be true. To many, the needed weight to shed off if they must achieve purpose is to keep some flocks of friends far away from them.

Weights have always appeared appealing and attractive to human but only those who have the understanding will know that the end thereof is destruction. The wife of pharaoh gave Joseph an attractive offer but he was sensible enough to discern that this weight is capable of distracting my destiny. The bible says he fled. Comparing Samson and Joseph; what Joseph allowed to let go was what the Samson absorbed to enjoy. Of course, we know where and how they both ended their purpose in life. Which do you want? Think about these!

I know sometimes it is hard to let go of the things of the world or those who are dearest to our hearts. Many at times, it is hard to take up our cross and follow Christ daily because of the fear that if we do so, we will lose the people around us, but that is where we must have faith and trust that everything will be okay. It is so sure that the moments you decide to follow Christ you will lose people even close pals. See! If this is your case, it shows you are doing the right thing. You can't claim to follow Christ and everything still remains the same way they used to be, never! *2 Corinthians 5:17 says "if any man be in Christ, he is a new creature, old things are passed away behold all things are become new"*(KJV). So it is certain that men will despise you and you may possibly lose some group of friends but I must tell you, if this is what is needed for you to focus on your purpose then I can say, it's worth it. They (pals with the old life) will leave you even if you seem not to send them off, why? It's due to the fact that, when a man changes kingdom many things change about such person, the language, choice of words, actions, understanding of life, perception about things, where not to go change over time. So many things change when you follow Christ. All I can say here is that you should prepare yourself for the restructuring (change). When God was to choose Abraham, he told him to leave his father's house where they were sacrificing to idols. He changed his location for him to fulfil his God's given purpose. There is always a setting apart for a man who will fulfil purpose.

One of the hardest things a young Christian will have to do is to let go of some of the people we love the most. These people may be the closest to our heart and ones whom we thought or think we can never live without. This may be for various reasons such as; they are bad company, unsaved, simple pulling us down spiritually and they are in place in our lives where they are not supposed to be. For example, there may be a so-called boyfriend or girlfriend, in which one is hoping, will be our future husband or wife. But Spirit of God is just saying 'no He or She is not the one'.

Now in a situation like that, it is and will be very heart breaking. One of the worst feelings in the world, where we may feel as if we can't go on or feel as if God has disappointed us, but we must have the understanding that God knows best. Just because we can't see in the future doesn't mean that God cannot. He knows it all; He is the beginning and the end. The bible states in Jeremiah 29:11 that "God has a plan and a purpose for our lives, not to harm us but to give us hope and a future".[2] What could be so amazing than the Creator guiding our steps? Nothing can compare. The fact that Christ is in control of our lives should give us as young Christians hope about our future.

I know that we can become fearful of the decisions that we have to make as young followers of Christ. Often times, we are worried about what people will think of us. Besides, along the journey we will end up losing friends or even have family that will disagree with us. Nevertheless, we have to look past all that and allow Christ to have is way in our lives. One thing that is certain and that is if we continuously worry about what people will think of us is that we will never be able to fulfil our purpose in Christ Jesus.

---

[2] Jer. 29.11 For I know the thoughts that I think toward you, saith the Lord, thoughts of peace, and not of evil, to give you an expected end.

The fear of what people will say has put so many destinies in quick graves. Men over time have always had things to say and that is why we are human. When we see changes, we tend to react to them, either good or bad. The fear of what people will say should not be enough reason why you should relent or stop following Christ.

It will amaze you to know that when God was about delivering the Israelites from Egypt using Moses, the children of Israelites cried to Moses saying 'you should have left us, so that our punishment will be minimal as usual. Now that you claim to deliver us, pharaoh has increased our tasks and it's now more difficult. Leave us alone in this slavery'.

When God delivered them and they got to the red sea, they shouted at Moses again, saying; why have your God brought us to die in the red sea, you should have left us to be slaves in Egypt. If people (Israelites) kept talking against God in spite of several powers and wonders he did in Egypt and even for delivering them, then who are you for men not to talk about you. Again I will beseech you to prepare for it, because it's certain, it (rejection from men) will come if you haven't experience one.

If we keep on looking back and giving things more value than our God, then we will never be able to live a fulfilled life.

Scroll, select and delete; that is what we ought to do sometimes. The bible says in *Romans16; 17 "Now I beseech you, brethren, mark them which causes divisions and offenses contrary to the doctrine which you have learned and avoid them". (KJV)* Obeying the above scripture takes a serious, dogged and a rugged determination.

Sometimes it might take God telling you to resign from the office where you render service to earn your living and be a full time evangelist. To some, God can instruct them to break the relationship, which was proposed to lead to marriage. The scripture in Romans 16:17 give the criteria for selecting and deleting people from the list. What are the criteria to watch out for? People with different belief and ideas to God's word, they are expected to be deleted from your friends list.

The scriptures say according to *2 Corinthians 6:14 "Be ye not unequally yoked with unbelievers..."* With the above scriptures I hope by now you have a clear knowledge of things, or people that must leave your list and those who should remain.

Delete those who God says to let go of, yes memories will still be there and we will be reminded of the past very often; of how things used to be and feelings that we are missing out on and so the pain will be there for a period of time that's for sure, but His grace is sufficient and what he brings you to, He will bring you through. If we get so caught up in the love of God and a close relationship with Christ, we will be filled with his love that our past become trivial and we can easily begin to move on to fulfil our purposes.

We have more or less heard the saying that 'Sometimes God calms the storm. Sometimes, he lets the storm rage and calms his child'. Perhaps, He is doing the same thing in your life and you may not understand why you are going through the trials and struggles. That's where faith steps in, if we trust in God and obeys him then we can be assured that the outcome will be a great one. That you and I will not be victims but rather victors, the head and not the tail, the lender and not barrower.

Those who were great in the bible had to either struggle for a while, loose something or give up something in order for them to walk into their destiny or become blessed and purified. Take for example; Joseph was a slave for many years before he became the prince of Egypt. Hannah too prayed at Shiloh for several years before she got her Samuel. Esther also was a slave in the land before she became the queen. David was a bush boy forgotten in the forest tending his father's sheep until he became a king. Hear this! Only tough people get going during tough times. Tough time doesn't last but tough people do. Listen to this! When the road looks TOUGH, it's because it is the way to the TOP. Many who have accomplished destiny went the rough way before coming the smooth way.

The scriptures did not say there wouldn't be storm but God gave us the assurance of victory. *Psalm 30:5b says "weeping might endure for a night, but joy cometh in the morning" (KJV).* Don't panic, don't be afraid. The beginning might not look like it but hopefully the end will fully form to the image someday.

Look around you, is there anyone who keeps

on saying 'that they went through fire, swam across the ocean and I made it because God kept me'? If your answer is yes or even no, then it is time for you to become a testimony too.

It is time for us, young Christians to stand our Ground and say to ourselves daily 'I am not giving up, I do not care what the world thinks, or what those on the outside is doing, I will follow Jesus until the end'. Of course that is easier said than done because of the generation we are living in. If we leave too far from home, as in, we leave the area of godly people around us then our lives spiritually decrease. The reason is that 99% of the people around us are not saved and this can make a bad influence on us. I speak for myself here 'the music in shops is worldly, movies too, and when I go to visit different places, I hear and see things that are ungodly. Also, that I have unsaved friends and family, for sure if I spend more time with them than with God and godly people, I'll find my faith decreasing and also my spiritual life'.

Hebrews 11:6 'Without faith it is impossible to please God....' and without faith it is impossible to fulfil your purpose in God.

Don't be afraid of what you see; be confident in what you know. Jesus said blessed are those who have not seen but have believed. It may happen that the spirit of God told you to do something, but you keep on asking questions such as; why me? What will they think? What will the outcome be? Stop doubting, just have faith in Jesus. I hear many people when they say "I trust myself", "I know what I can do" and "what I can't do". I just smile at such statements. Listen well and good! You don't know yourself and don't trust yourself. You should only trust God because your flesh can fail you. Man is limited. Only God is trustworthy. What if I tell you that your eyes can deceive you, do you believe that?

Numbers 13:26-33, talked on the account of how Moses sent 12 spies to go search out the land of Canaan. On the arrival of the 12 spies, 10 of them came with evil report. Why was it evil report? It was evil report because they believed what their eyes saw. They said the inhabitants of the land are giants and muscular. Yes! This is true but for them to have said **'we all looked like a grasshopper before them'** was where the 10 spies missed it all. Why did they speak with such level of fear; they allowed their own eyes to deceive

34

them. In the midst of this all, came 2 other spies, which said **'we are able to overcome them'**. All the 12 spies saw the giants with their eyes but 2 out of 12 believed in their heart that they are able. It is therefore deceptive and confusing to obey and follow what our eyes sees. There is more to this physical sight, children of the kingdom engage their heart not just their eyes. Have faith in God; again I say have faith in God.

'Go' by Mali Music is one my favourite songs and it really encourages me. 'I see where this road is taking me but my soul gets so heavy but the Spirit says go.' The song always reminds me that it does not matter Whether or not we see where the road is taking us we should still go. If the Spirit says go just go.

If the God that we serve is the beginning and the end, then for sure we have to trust him. You see, the more we focus on the things we have to let go of, the more we become consumed by it and it makes us lose focus of what is the right thing to do. Instead, we should fix our eyes on the prize that is set before us. Whatever you see catches your attention and whatever you hear determines your decision. The question to you is; who have you been looking at and whom have you been hearing from? Listen to this! "Who you look at, you look like". That's what I call the principle of reflection.

The scripture in 1Corinthians 3:18 says "But *we all, with open faces beholding as in a glass the glory of the Lord, ARE CHANGED into the same image from GLORY to GLORY'. (KJV)*. Prior to the verse, they were changed into the image of God as they behold him. They got transformed from glory of men into the glory of God. This change happened just by beholding. Can you now agree that who you look at is what you look like? When you look at your worries, you'll look like them. When you look at your problems, you will look like them. Why not look at Jesus the Author and Finisher of your faith.

Jonathan nelson sings a song 'called to be' and from my perspective it is also a declaration. 'I will be what you call me to be I say yea'. Now looking into the words it makes me realise that I will only become what I am called to be if and only if I say yes to God. So go on say yes and Amen. No point if I sit and say oh I've been called to be a leader, a preacher, prophet, evangelist, an usher, administrator, if all I do is sit and do nothing. I must make steps to further the vision if going to accomplish my assignment on this planet earth, if it means letting go of some friends then let them go, if it means staying up to pray, then let sleep go. Go on; let it go; say it out loud to yourself; let it go!'

Whatever vision it is God has given to you, nothing happens until you take action. Action is what makes vision a reality. Until you do something about it, GOD will do nothing about it. It's time to be decisive and intentional in your choice if you must fulfil purpose in life. Can you listen to this! "Principles are what people followed closely that made them a principal in the field" when you have mastered a principle so much and given yourself to it, you become a subject matter in such field. Why? It's simply because whatever a man believes, he becomes. *John1:12says "But as many as RECEIVED (BELIEVED) Him, to them gave He the power to BECOME the sons of GOD" ... (KJV)*

When I say let go and let God this means that in every way possible Christ must have his way. The bible states that the spirit is willing but my flesh is weak. We all know what it feels like when the flesh kicks in and wants to have its own way. I remember my youth group had a prayer meeting and one of the youth leaders said 'if God gives a word then speak'. I sat down not looking up and the Spirit of God was speaking and I was like 'no way am I speaking'. Now the flesh was also speaking to me' what if what you say is not from God, sit down someone else will speak'. I was getting stressed out and it wasn't until it became a burden on my heart before I began to speak. It was indeed from the spirit and what I spoke to a young lady she confirmed that it was true. You see if we listened to the flesh and the carnal mind, we will never do what is required.

Allowing God takes faith and courage, and it's not easy. But if it were easy everyone would do it. Remember many are called and chosen are few.

Believing God and obeying God could be slightly different. Yes! Different, many believe Jesus is the son of God, they believe Jesus died for our sins, they believed in the trinity (God the father, the son and the Holy Spirit), they believe so many other things about God but obeying him as been a war in their flesh.

Can you imagine someone slapped you and didn't feel guilty of anything and God told you to go and reconcile with the person and forgive the person, smiles! How convenient is it for you to obey? Quite tough, right? What about God telling you to empty your account for a church project. How easy is it for you to eagerly and willingly obey the almighty? A great deal right?

What exactly does it mean to allow God?

• It means submitting your will to his will. As a matter of fact, believers don't have self-will but the will of the father only.

• It means to humble yourself under the authority of God. James5: 'humble yourself before the lord, and he shall exalt you in due time' the scripture says 'God resists the proud'. If you must allow God, then you must be humble. Humble means, "thinking less of yourself".

• It means to recognise God. That is, to acknowledge Him. *Proverbs 3:5-6 says "Trust in the lord with all your heart and lean not on your own understanding. In all your ways acknowledge Him and he shall direct your path."*

(KJV)

Whatever you commit in the hands of God, you will see the hands of God in it. When you commit yourself to someone, you allow the person to take charge over you. In same sense, when a man commits himself to God, he his invariably saying "Lord I surrender all to you"

A songwriter sings "I surrender all to you. Everything I give to you, withholding nothing it takes a mature Christian to sing that song and be committed to it. Many people can surrender their things and materials to God but find it difficult to surrender themselves. The song says withholding nothing, including yourself. This was the state Abraham met himself when he was tested by God that he should go and offer his only son Isaac as a sacrifice. It could be so painful and sacrificial releasing your only son, but Abraham obeyed God. Have you gotten to a level where you can't withhold anything from God?

Scripture in Matthew 19:16-23 gives the account of a rich young man who wanted to follow Christ and have eternal life. Jesus told him if you must have eternal life then you must keep my commandment; thou shall not commit adultery, thou shall not commit murder, thou shall not steal and thou shall not bear false witness but the young rich man said I do all these you said even from my youth.

At a certain point Jesus told the young rich man, do this last one and then follow me and be my disciples. Guess what? Jesus told him, sell all that you have and give them all to the poor. The bible says that the young rich man went home sorrowful because he could not release them as instructed by Jesus. Many of us are in the shoe of this young rich man. We can come for all church services, clean the church, go on evangelism but when the pastor says let's make a sacrificial seed to a project in church, your countenance changes. Your money can hardly be counted in any of the church projects with your long years of being a member why? Could it be that you are just like the rich man who can't release all to Jesus withholding nothing?

Another song that I love to worship with is I give myself away. The words are just beautiful ' my life is not my own to you I belong I give myself to you'. Every time I hear this song I weep because I want to give my all to God and also I

41

think of all that must and have given up for my faith. It won't be easy but it will be worth it. Cliff quotes "many rivers to cross, but in this case I will find my way over to Jesus' path".

Let me share this hilarious story with you; a young man who is an unbeliever had a prompting in his heart to go to church. On getting to church, the pastor made an altar call and the young man gave his life to Christ as he was deeply touched by the pastor's message. Subsequently, when it was time to give offering, out of the abundance of excitement from the heart of this young man that he is saved, he emptied his pocket into the offering basket. On his way home, some gangsters stopped him, brought out a gun and told him "your money or your life". And he laughed as he replied the robbers "I don't have any". The robbers were shocked and they asked him what do you mean, he told them I gave my life to Christ today therefore my life is with Christ. As per the money, I emptied my pocket in the basket too. The robbers laughed and they said because you have made us laugh we go to church with you someday. That was how he was rescued. The young man gave his all that day to Christ (his money and his life). What are you still withholding from God? What is that thing that still looks too big for you to release to God?

You have to remind yourself each and every day that I will stand firm, like Prodigal Son says 'a radical soldier'. I must I shall win this battle. I am reminder that it is a set battle and I have already won. I will do my best and God will do the rest, I will do the natural and he will do the supernatural'.

Walk into your destiny by faith and obedience to the word of God. The fulfilment of your purpose is only determined by your obedience of the word of God. Make your dreams of a powerful child of God become a reality, you are wonderful, powerful, beautiful yes and you are more than capable of letting go of the things that's keep pulling you back from fulfilling your purpose in life, you have the ability to do all things in Christ Jesus our Lord.

There's a general saying that "when the purpose of a thing is unknown, abuse is inevitable". How true is this saying? Very true! Many have lived their lives wastefully and carelessly because they are ignorant of God's purpose for their lives. Hear this! The purpose of life is to live a life of purpose. Please follow me closely on this short story of a little boy and his mother.

The mother of a little boy was to go out for a while and on her departure she locked up all the rooms, both the kitchen and everywhere and her son was left in the corridor outside but before the mother left, she gave her son a booklet and instructed him to read it all.

The questions that pops up to the son remains; mum didn't give me food, mum didn't give me chocolate, she didn't even give me keys to the living room to watch the TV so I can always keep myself busy by seeing a movie before her arrival. She only gave me a booklet. For what! In that anger he threw the booklet away.

Many thoughts popped through the mind of the little boy. Why will my mom do this to me, she has been loving, caring and kind to me ever since I was born, could she have changed so suddenly? Two of the friends of the little boy came around and shared their experiences. One said the last time his parents went out, they gave him access to everywhere in the house except his dad's room, which was locked. The little boy asked his friends, why were you not given access to your dad's room. The friend answered, so many precious things are in my dad's room and they don't want me to touch them at all.

The second friend also shared a similar story that his dad's room is always locked whenever his parents are not around, and they concluded to the little boy by saying, 'your mom is wicked and she doesn't love you'. Right in the centre of their discussion, the mom of the little boy arrived and the boy shouted mummy why? Mummy why? And she asked, "What is it"? The boy said to his mom, you didn't give me access to the house keys, you only gave me a booklet which was not relevant to what I needed so I threw it away The mother laughed and she said all you need to access the house is in the booklet. How do you mean mom? Asked the little boy. The mom answered, I gave you the booklet because that's the manual that contains everything in this house, I mean everything, even the place where the house key is kept, is also in the booklet The little boy screamed oh my God!

The little boy went further and asked the mom why didn't you give me the keys directly instead of the booklet? The mother replied, I gave you the booklet so I can always relate my mind with you personally also and for security reasons, because the key to your dad's room is also in the bunch of keys. The mother concluded I have only devised a means to give my darling son all that is in this house and also help him secure it in his hands. wow! The little boy and his friends gave applause to the mother.

What message can you infer from this story, dear reader.

1. The mother represents God

2. The little boy represents a believer

3. The two friends represent the world

4. The booklet which gives access to the house represents the word of God which gives access to the kingdom.

5. Ignorance is deadly. That you don't know your purpose doesn't mean you don't have one. The scripture says "my people perish because of lack of knowledge".

Listen to this! God does not waste resources and therefore he can't create you for nothing. You are created for a purpose. The life you have is for a purpose. Friends can confuse you into believing that God has forgotten you, just like the friends confused the little boy that his mom is wicked. Friends are not the one who created you and that's why they can't know your purpose. God alone knows the purpose for which he created you. While man can also know the purpose for which he was created by the word of God.

God gave us power and authority; therefore, it will be an error if we don't exercise them. Don't be overwhelmed by the challenges around you, there's a purpose for it. Don't be carried away by worries, remember there's a purpose. Your friends might be making it in their field and therefore asking you to compromise your stand if you must make it like them. Just let them know there's a purpose for the moment. God is too organised to disorganise your life. In all the ups and down, just know that there's a purpose. Be focused, don't wave, be strong and be yielding as you see the clearer picture of your purpose in a brighter way.

CHAPTER 1

WHAT IS HUMAN NATURE?

For over many centuries, the question of human nature has been one of the most unanswerable questions, none of us seems to have the answer; it is a mystery that neither science nor religion can break down for us even until this day. This particular question has left a lot of human beings in desolation. Science has told us that humans are animals, evolved beings with evolved bodies and evolved minds, which don't seem to make any sense to many of us.

I remember on this particular day I was sitting outside Costa with my friends having a drink and so I began to tell them about the love of God and how important we are all to Him. One of them responded by saying that she "don't believe in the whole God thing and that Man evolved from monkey's". I politely answered her with a question; I asked her, "Do you have a boyfriend?" and she answered, "yes," I then asked her, "Do you truly love him?" "Yes," she responded and I asked her, "Would you tell your boyfriend that you truly love that he evolved from a monkey?" She said, "No I wouldn't say that because that wouldn't be appropriate." Then I said, "There you go, that just cancelled your evolution." She was astonished how I portrayed it to her and made her reflect that human beings evolving from monkeys cannot be true. Even though some of this theory about evolution was developed and proposed by a man called Charles Darwin. His theory has had a great influence on science and the way there understand life and see the world. Darwin was the first to develop a conceivable, natural source for the process of evolution as a scientist and naturalist. He once identified himself as a Christian, but as a result of some tragedies that took place in his life, then he later renounced the Christian faith and the existence of God and that led him in a journey of gradually disputing about Christianity and the bible not being the true divine revelation. Paul S. Taylor, (Christian Answer) stated that "Darwin's unbelief, like that of so many people today, had its roots in a mind which first rejected the revelation of God in the Bible and then was unwilling to accept the revelation of God, which God Himself has given in nature. This revelation, of the Bible, of the Lord Jesus Christ, will keep us tuned to truth, hope, and life in God, and away from evolutionism, humanism, and atheism, only as we allow it to exercise its power in our hearts. The tragedy of Charles Darwin is that he never did". Some of us today are like Darwin, we not allowing the gospel of the kingdom of God to transform our hearts then after we complain about why the world is in so much desolation, life is so tough and bad things is keep on happening on the earth. You see you can only experience the revelation of God if you allow its power to transform your heart and to enable you to see the bigger picture of why God created mankind and put them in this planet. But many of us are not doing that and we wonder why we are in so much confusion about the creation.

The fact of the matter is that many human beings on this planet are trying to discover this mystery called "HUMAN NATURE" but it seems as if we are looking into the wrong places and resources. If we are truly willing to discover this mystery of human nature, we are obligated to look at the company that manufactured it. For example, if I want to discover something about Mercedes Benz, I wouldn't go to Audi to try to find the exact information that I need to know about Mercedes-Benz, because that's not the company that manufactured it. If I do, I am likely to get the wrong information because I'm in the wrong company. The late Dr Myles Munroe quoted "The truth of a product it's hidden in the manufacturer." Only the manufacturer knows the full truth about his product.

So for us to know the full truth about the human nature we first need to consult the manufacturer who made it, or otherwise we will just be going round in circles. Only the person who made it knows the truth about His product. And every manufacturer who creates a product always sends with it an instruction manual that takes us on a journey of how the product functions. But sadly most of us don't read the instruction manual that comes with the product because we think that we can use the product without the instructions, that's why when it malfunctions we don't know what to do with it and we may take it to the wrong manufacturer to try and get it fixed. That's when the problem gets worst because the company that we have taken it to lacks the necessary skills to fix the product. **"To get an effective result of a product, you first need to discover the manufacturer that made it"**. **The manufacturer's mind is as important as the product itself, because what we call the product was first pictured in the mind of the manufacturer. Therefore, a product can't say for itself, "this is the purpose for which it was created". A man cannot also say this is why he was created until he acknowledges that there's someone who is responsible for his making, and thereby need to go and ask few questions about his life (product). A product used without the manufacturer instruction cannot stand the test of time.** Now let us discover the manufacturer of the human nature.

CHAPTER 2

HUMAN NATURE MANUFACTURER

The first thing that we need to know about the manufacturer of the human nature is that He is a SUPREME Being and He lives in an another realm world called the "Spiritual" world. Which most of us are not familiar with, because we are used to the natural world called earth and that includes everything we see around us, the sky, the grass, houses, your own body, other people and much more. Now let's define the spiritual world.

WHAT IS A SPIRITUAL WORLD?

The simple definition that I can come up with

is this; "the spiritual world is the world that consists of the unseen realities that we do not fully encounter until after death".[3]

This Supreme Being who lives in an unseen world, He is eternal, and for us to be able to communicate with Him about His product we need to fight that which constrains us.[4] The first instruction that is given to us as the way forward in discovering the Supreme Being is "belief", we first need to believe that He exists. Believing that he exists is how you are going to find Him, because from believing comes knowing and from knowing comes the conviction of the heart is that, knowing that He truly exists without a shadow of a doubt. The scripture says 'with heart man believes unto righteousness but with mouth confession is made unto salvation'. Since God cannot be physically seen with our naked eyes, cannot be touched with our bare hands; how then do we communicate and access this God. The very first step is to believe Him. The whole Christian

---

[3]Hebrew 11:1 now faith is the assurance of things hope for, the conviction of things not seen. (NIV)

2 Corinthians 4:18 So we fix our eyes not on what is seen, but on what is unseen, since what is seen is temporary, but what is unseen is eternal. (NIV)

[4]Hebrews 11:6 It is impossible to please God without faith. Anyone who wants to come to him must believe that God exists and that he rewards those who sincerely seek him. (NIV)

race is all about believing. We were not on earth when the bible was written, we were not born when Jesus was going about with his disciples. We were not born when several things in the bible happened, but we connect to these happenings by believing and we saw them practically happened. We read how Jesus healed people miraculously in the bible, we also believe it and prayer are made for people and we see the same kind of miracle happen again. This alone is an indication that the Bible is not just a book but also a living entity. We hereby conclude that the relationship of any man with God is based on the level of his faith in God. The scriptures say Abraham believed God and it was counted unto him for righteousness. Believing is the key. How can you explain laying hands on the sick and the sick instantly getting recovered? All these could happen under the scope of belief. You cannot approach something that you don't believe exists, you will be trying to discover where water comes from without believing there are oceans that provide it. So if we are eager to try to find out about the human nature then we must also be eager to believe that God exists, to get any answers concerning this situation.[5]

The answer to all your questions is not far from you, but close to you. For it only takes one call to get all your answers and only God can answer all these questions concerning the human nature. When God created His product and called it "HUMAN" He made it just like any other manufacturer. He didn't just transmit His product without the instruction manual. But He made sure that He sent it with the appropriate instructions, so that we would not get carried away whilst trying to figure out how the product is made and its functions.

He made it comprehensible in His instruction manual, it contains all the information that we need about His product. Furthermore, the bible states, "I am the Vine, you are the branches. He who abides in Me, and I in him. Bears much fruit; for without Me you can do nothing".[6] Thus, God is simply saying that, humans cannot function adequately without Him in our lives.

The scripture "without me you can do nothing" is very loaded and should be a reason

---

[5]Jeremiah 29:13, you will seek me and find me when you seek me with all your heart. (NIV)
[6](John 15:4,5-6.). (NIV)

enough for people to desire GOD intimately. What the scripture mean in a plain term is; if you must live a life of purpose and a life worth living, then you must follow my instructions, because he that gives the "VISION" also has the "PROVISION". Stop the trial and error to be sure if GOD truly lives or not. Stop doing things outside the word of God for humanity. Stop trying to humanly calculate the things of the spirit. GOD did it so good that he didn't put us in darkness or confusion of our purpose but provided a study-guide for us to follow. In other words, if this product is going to be understood and function in its purpose, it only needs to go back to the hands of the one who created it and that is GOD. In the same wise, the more you study the manual, the more you know how best to use the product and understand the purpose of the product. Can i tell you that there's more to what you know. Accordingly, now let me take you on a journey of discovering the making of human nature according to God's manual.

THE CREATION OF HUMAN NATURE

God's instruction manual tells us a great deal

about the creation of mankind's human nature. God began the production process of His product just like any other producer. First, he started by analyzing the "environment", he knew that the environment must be suitable for the product and if the environment were not satisfactory then the product would be deemed ineffective. Thus, the product would not function the way that the creator intended for it to be. (Genesis 1:1, 27)

WHAT IS ENVIRONMENT?

Some scholars define the environment as the "surrounding or conditions in which a person, animal or a plant lives, grows, develops and operates".[7] If the surroundings or conditions of the environment are not in its best state, then the product will fail. For example, it can be argued that the economy of countries across the world is failing because it is not the way God intended it to be.

Moreover, there are so many problems across the world, the domain of countries are in a state of flux. Consequently, we are looking for a solution,

---

[7]M Rajamanickam, *Modern General Psychology, Second Edition (revised and Expanded) (in 2 Vols.)* (Concept Publishing Company 2007) 92

but yet still many of us fail to openly admit that we need help. *A problem can only be solved where there is honesty, and where there is no honesty, there is no dignity, and only God can give us dignity if we are honest that we need Him to intervene.* According to God, when he created His product He named it "human" and it was pleasing unto Him.[8]

After creating the environment and everything in it, God was still unsatisfied because there was no one to rule over it all. A manufacturer doesn't just create a product without a purpose, God created the world, as a suitable environment for the personal use of His product to function in a safe and productive way. Here is what Gods manual state concerning the environment in the book of *Genesis 2:5. "And no plant of the field had appeared on the earth, and no herb of the field had sprung up, for the LORD GOD had not caused it to rain upon the earth, and there was not a MAN to till the ground." (KJV)*

God did not allow anything to function in the environment that He created because there was no product to work the material that He had

---

[8] Genesis 1:31, God saw all that he had made, and it was very good. And there was evening, and there was morning- the sixth day. (NIV)

made. As a manufacturer, He created an environment for the sake of His product; there was a need for the environment to be replenished and for the product to benefit from it. As a result, God did not just create the environment for Him to look at but for His product to benefit from. In simple terms, *the earth was created for the benefit of human beings to enjoy everything in it.* It is highly important and essential to know that environment is the basis of survival and how lasting a product will be. The environment is capable of determining the life span of a product. How do I mean? The bible talked about the parable of the sower. How some seed fell on rock, some fell within thorns and some fell on a fertile ground. This is a biblical narration of the same seed in different environment. Only the seed that fell on the fertile soil was said to stand the test of time and blossom, while the other seeds died along the line. In other words, environment goes a long way in determining the sustainability of the product.

Let me give you another scripture in reference to Environment. *Psalm 1:3 states "And he shall be like a tree planted by the rivers of water that brings forth its fruit in its season; his leaf shall not wither and whatsoever he does shall prosper"*. If you check and study that scripture closely, the reason why there is fruit in due season is not because the seed is super but because the seed is planted in a favourable environment that suits it. Suitable environment is not a choice in life but a necessity. Now let us take a look at the process of developing His product, us, me and you.

CHAPTER 3

THE PROCESS OF HUMAN

It is crucial to give full attention to the instructions of a product, as a result of focusing on the details you will uncover what the product is made of. For example, Genesis 2:6, 7 "but streams came up from the earth and watered the whole surface of the ground. Then the LORD God formed the MAN from the dust of the ground. He breathed the breath of life into the man's nostrils, and the man became a living person." These scriptures help us to understand how mankind was created and our environment.

This particular description in the instruction manual is showing us how God began the process of His product called "human". It tells us that

God formed "MAN" from the dust of the ground and He breathed the breath of life into the man's nostril. It is of great value to first identify the reason as to why God used the dust of the ground to form a man before He breathed the breath of life into him. In spite of the fact that with the rest of the creation, He spoke it into existence. In Genesis 1:3, 14, 20, 24, God simply spoke everything into existence, but when it came to creating man He did things differently.

Perhaps many of you may very well be asking yourselves why God made "MAN" out of the dust of the ground. (Genesis 2:7). Great, let me tell you more. The fact that God created man out of the dust of the ground is because God wanted something unique and different in the middle of all His creation. So He used a different way to create Man to convey that distinctiveness from all of His creation.

The Bible says that to create the sun, mountains, trees, birds and animal life and much more God purely spoke them into existence, "Then God said" See (Genesis 1:3, 14, 20, 24), but when it came to human life, He, incorporated the "Dust of the ground" and the extraordinary breath of God Almighty Himself. Such a mode of creation highlights the importance and value of human life.[9] The use of dust represents certain lowliness. As we have read, God did not use gold or granite or gemstones to create man, but He used simple dust, a humble substance to create His product, "human." (Genesis 3:19) Now let us define what a human is.

WHAT IS A HUMAN?

Like you, this question has been one of my major concerns; I was once longing to know what a human being is made of. I believe that to be able to fully commit to the role that God has called you to play in this life, you must become aware of your identity in the first place. Speaking from experience, over the past few years, I have been trying to discover my identity as a means of becoming satisfied. There is an unsatisfied part in every human being that cannot be satisfied by earthly things.

Throughout the process of this research, I discovered that the word "human" is a

---

[9]Genesis 2:7 Then the LORD God formed a man from the dust of the ground and breathed into his nostrils the breath of life, and the man became a living being.

combination of two words put together "EARTH" and "SPIRIT". The word "HUMAN" comes from a Latin word "HUMUS", which means EARTH or GROUND and the word MAN, is a Hebrew word "ISH" which means SPIRIT. Therefore, a human is a mixture of two words put together HUMUS – MAN that we pronounce human. Bishop Abel Kungu says, *"A human is a spirit being, possessing a soul and living in a body"*.

Here it is telling us that when God created man, He first did a mixture of the dust of the ground, and then after He breathed into his nostrils the breath of life, and he became a living soul. This verse is very critical because it reveals to us the making of a human; he came out of God himself, so it shows us that a human being is a duplicate of God. God himself birthed him, He came out of God's own Spirit because God intended this human that He created ought to operate on His level and so He made man just like Him in His own personal image. Hence, a human doesn't have a spirit, he is a spirit that came out of God to live according to the way that he was created to live and that is JUST LIKE GOD.

On that account, the unfulfilled desire that's in

the heart of humans can never be truly filled, least not by another human being or by any earthly possessions. In the view of the fact that you and I were not created to live or function without God, our Source. For example, fishes were not created to live without water or otherwise they will malfunction and die. To murder a fish, you don't need to kill it, you just have to disconnect it from its environment and it will die. Another example, to kill a flower you just have to disconnect it from the sun and it will die. These two things thrive when connected to their environment.

Key Quotations Regarding Humans

➤ *A Human is an incorporation of earthly and heavenly at the same time.*

➤ *A 'Human" is a unique combination of earthly, natural material and life giving power from God Himself.*

➤ *A Human is a spirit being who happens to live in a dirt body.*

Correspondently, the same principle applies to every human concerning this burning malcontent desire in our heart. It can only be actualized in each of us individually when we are connected back to our Source, which is God the Creator, as our perfection is found only in Him. *Unless a human is connected back to its original source that fulfilment will always be in our hearts.* Henceforth, let us discover the purpose of this human that is made in the Image of God.

THE PURPOSE OF THE HUMAN NATURE

UNLOCKED

Everything in life has a purpose. Each one of us was born with and for a purpose. It is whilst we are living according to our purpose that we can find ourselves living a meaningful life. Without purpose, this life has no meaning at all. For where purpose is not known life is just an experiment or chaotic journey that results in frustration, disappointment and failure. Without purpose, life is subjective; it is a game of trial and error, which is ruled by environmental influences and the circumstances of the moment. Likewise, in the absence of purpose, time has no meaning, energy has no reason and life has no precision. Therefore, it is essential that we understand and discover our purpose in life so that we can experience an effective, full and satisfying life.

Before we can explore the discovery of the purpose of human nature, it is necessary for us to first discover the authentic meaning of the word "PURPOSE". Understanding the concept of the word may very well add greater clarity to our discussion and understanding.

Key Quotations Regarding the Nature of Humans

➤ "For until purpose is discovered, existence has no meaning, for purpose is the source of fulfilment".[10] Says Dr. Myles Munroe

➤ "Without God, life has no purpose, and without purpose, life has no meaning. Without meaning, life has no significant or hope".[11] Says Rick Warren

➤ "For nothing is created without purpose". Says Bishop Abel Kungu

---

[10] In pursuit of purpose, Dr Myles Monroe
[11] The Purpose Driven Life, Rick Warren

WHAT IS PURPOSE?

According to the Oxford Dictionary, Purpose is the reason for which something is done or created or for which something exists.

For example, the purpose of a chair is for individuals to sit down on, While, the purpose of a house is to have a home to live in. In other words, the fruition of a product is to know when it is to be used for its proper purposes.

During my explorations of this subject, I discovered that PURPOSE is the following:

➤ The original intent for the creation of a thing,

➤ The original reason for the existence of a thing,

➤ The cause for the creation of a thing,

➤ The need that makes a manufacturer produces a specific production,

➤ The destination that prompts the journey,

➤ The end for which the means exist,

➤ The why that explains the reason for existence

➤ The desired result that initiates production.

Purpose, therefore, is the original intent in the mind of the creator that motivated him to create a specific product. In other words, before the making of any product, there is a purpose established in the mind of the manufacturer that gives conception to the idea that becomes the matter for the design and production of the product. Therefore, purpose precedes production, *Jeremiah 1:5 states "Before I formed thee in the belly I knew thee and before you came out of your mother's womb I sanctified thee and ordained you a prophet to the nation" (KJV).* Purpose is the foundation of any production. The purpose of Christ has been prophesied by several prophets in the Old Testament of the Bible far before his physical birth in the New Testament. Whatever you see in existence at all has a purpose. Whatever it is you don't know the purpose is because you haven't discovered it. Life remains worth living and interesting when it is in purpose. Every product is produced on purpose and for a purpose, nothing in this world is produced without a reason. Every product exists to satisfy the original purpose for which it was created. The existence of a thing has no meaning until its purpose is discovered.

Growing up as a young child in Africa I struggled with this question, "What is my purpose?" Like many of you, I asked myself several questions, am I just here to live for a little while and accept everything that life throws at me and die. I couldn't get my head around it, there was a longing in me to understand why I was born. Was I just here to get rich or famous and then die? I often told myself "No", there has to be more to life.

During my younger years, I and those around me somehow saw me as a peculiar individual. One, who did not live up to the expectations of those within society, and thus I was burdened with questions regarding my existence. I believe that you who are reading this book right now, you may be struggling with the same questions in your mind. Why am I here? Am I here just to pay bills and die? From now on, I want you to start saying to yourself, *"No, I was born for greater works than this"*.

On the road of my researching and yearning to discover the purpose of my existence, I met up with a Man who claimed to be the Son of God, a

Man who the Bible talks about. He came to earth to die for the sins of humanity and to reintroduce the purpose of their existence, to give them a sense and a purpose of living. I was so excited and eager to know this man personally. When I found Him I completely surrendered all my life to Him and He changed me totally from the inside out and He helped me to discover the purpose of my existence. Life would have been purposeless and empty without Him, because He is the light of the world and without His presence the world would have been in gross darkness. He is the life that makes our life worth Living.

In Him was life and the life was the light of men. I couldn't just imagine myself being without life and without light. That's total catastrophe. I needed to reflect and ruminate deeply about the non-optional and the colossal necessity accepting Him. How would it have been for me to walk in darkness?

A man cannot appreciate light to its zenith measure of importance if it has not experience darkness in the high order. For instance, I was lodged in a room, suddenly the power supply was interrupted for about ten minutes, you wouldn't believe it that I was searching for my car key for that ten minutes, I couldn't find it. Suddenly, the light was restored; it was a great surprise for me only to discover that the car key was right beside me on the bed. For few minutes I kept laughing at myself. What a mess of me!

The ten minutes of darkness passed a great deal of message to me on the inside, which made me appreciate the essence of light to the maximum. In fact, it boosts my desire, zeal and passion to fasten and facilitate the commencement of my relationship with Him. Here are hit points on darkness that gave light a huge significance:

Firstly, I was in deep confusion. I was eagerly searching for the car key but it was with no focus and direction. A life that lives in darkness will have no focus and direction.

Secondly, the darkness brought about wasted time and effort. All the time I spent searching didn't yield the desired result. So is it for a life in darkness. Such people work so much with little or no reward. What I wasted ten minutes searching for was what I got in less than ten seconds. Darkness wastes people's lives and destinies.

Thirdly, the darkness brought about lack of

vision because the scripture says where there is no vision the people perish. While in the room, I couldn't picture anything at all, nothing was visible to me. Even though the car key was beside me, yet I couldn't find it because I had no vision. Though I have eyes, they couldn't see anything because there was darkness. Many cannot see the beauty and flavour in life because they have no vision.

All these, put together, made me see the exigencies of accepting the man who is light. Who brought me out of confusion, wasted time and effort, lack of vision and total darkness and brought me into the kingdom of light by sacrificing Himself. This man is called Jesus Christ of Nazareth.

He revealed to me the very thing I was searching and yearning for all my life as a young man and I have found it in Him alone and now "JESUS CHRIST is the only reason for my existence". I pray that as we continue to explore our purpose on this planet, that you will also rediscover the purpose of your existence and live an effective life every day. According, let's go on an expedition of rediscovering the reason for our existence together, shall we.

REDISCOVERING OUR PURPOSE

In the rediscovering of the reason for our existence, it is crucial to understand that before anything was, GOD is. The word "GOD" is not a name but rather a description of a character. Which simply means "Self - existing One or Self – sufficient One" and describes a being that needs nothing or no one to exist. Thus, because of whom He is and what He is, He alone qualifies for the title of God. This totally independent God existed before all things and began His creative process by first producing the entire invisible world, which we also have come to know as the "above" Spiritual world. This act of creation initiated the concept of "RULER" and "RULERSHIP" as the Creator became the Ruler over a created realm. Another word for a ruler is "KING." God called this invisible realm He had created 'HEAVEN' and therefore He Himself became the KING over the realm He named HEAVEN.

Yet still, I know many of you may still be asking yourselves the very same questions I once struggled with, 'Who is this God they all speak so highly of, who is the King over the realm of Heaven and why would he desire to create sons in His image on earth Was He not satisfied and pleased over the invisible realm of angels and powers to rule?' I believe the answer to these questions is first discovered in understanding the very nature and character of God Himself; revealed in His own personal instruction manual.

One of God's characteristics is revealed to us in 1 John 4:8, 16, it states that 'God is love'. Please note, it does not say that He "has" love but that He "Is" love. This is very important when it comes to understanding God's motivation. As a result of God being love, everything He does will naturally or supernaturally be the manifestation of the nature of love. I have discovered that two of the most obvious qualities of love is 'giving and sharing'. Therefore, the very nature of God requires Him to share His kingdom rulership and authority in spirit with his children through a relationship. Humankind was created for the very purpose of rulership and leadership through a relationship with God Himself, to rule the realm of the earth as God is ruling the realm of the invisible Heaven.

Moreover, in the book of Genesis, 1:26-27, God made a declaration concerning mankind. "And God said; Let us make man in our image, after our likeness: and let them have dominion over the fish of the sea, and over the birds of the air and over the livestock, and over all the earth, and over every creeping thing that creeps upon the earth. So God created man in His own image, in the image of God He created him, male and female He created them."

This very particular statement in the instruction manual of God is critical because it is the first declaration of God's intent for you and me. It encompasses the entire purpose of mankind in such significant and distinctive way that we should not question. It shows us the very motivation of what the manufacturer had in mind when He had a purpose of creating mankind in His own image and likeness. The statement covers the entire purpose, assignment, potential, passion and design of mankind as an entity. This statement is the key to mankind's natural desires, sense of purpose and fulfilment in life.

There are several of significant principles that are planted concerning the purpose of mankind in this first mission statement of God, concerning mankind's creation and this need to be carefully examined.

First principle:

Man was both created and made. The Bible uses two different Hebrew words in describing the creation of a mankind. Both of these words are distinctly different in the original Hebrew translation. The first word that is used is 'CREATED'; the definition of this word is 'BARA' in Hebrew, meaning to create from nothing. We see the example of this word Bara in Genesis 1:1 which says "In the beginning, God created (Bara) the heavens and earth," the use of this word indicates that God made heaven and earth out of nothing. The second word that is used is MAKE, the word ASAH in Hebrew, and which is translated to make or do something. Of course, when something is made it must be composed of pre-existing material. Therefore, mankind is the integration of parts that was created from nothing and things that were already made.

Therefore, the making of mankind is combined the very nature, attributes and characteristics of His Source, which is Elohim God the Creator Himself. This is really important to know when discussing the purpose of human nature. In my research, I also discovered that the word for 'SOURCE' in the original Hebrew language is the word "ABBA" which is translated as "FATHER" in English. Meaning that God sourced us all and therefore we possess His nature and likeness as Father of creation.

Second Principle:

Man was made in God's image. It is of great significance to know and understand the purpose of mankind, for the reason that if mankind is going to be successful and fulfilled in all of his doing there is a need to know their true identity and source. Thus, knowing that we are made in the very image of God Almighty Himself, is the truth we need.

The word "IMAGE" that is used here is not referring to physical likeness, but the Hebrew words Tselem and Demut, meaning, shadow, and the likeness of God, godlike characteristics, nature and essence. This indicates that man, as a spirit being is an expression of God's moral and spiritual nature and his attributes make him "godlike". Thus, mankind was created by God in the god-class and was given the responsibility to exercise that god-like characteristic on earth as God's own personal agent.

The word IMAGE means a replica of something or someone. If we are therefore created in the image of God, could it also mean that we can do whatever it is God does? Yes!

God did not make us like his shadows; he made us in His image. That is to show that we are not second class made beings but first class, exactly in the image of God. If He is light, it also means we are light. Scriptures states in *John 8:12 "Then spake Jesus again unto them saying, I am the light of the world; he that followeth me shall not walk in darkness, but shall have the light of life"*. This was Jesus saying here that He is the light of the world.

Moreover, if we also read through the book of *Matthew 5:14, "Ye are the light of the world, a city that is set on a hill, cannot be hidden"*. The word "Ye" as used in the scripture above refers to the children of God. We share the same nature and features with the father. If he is a light, also means that we are light.

Furthermore, we also share the same agenda, vision, purpose and drive. The scriptures state *1John 3:8b "For this purpose the son of man was made manifested that He might destroy the works of the devil". When we also look vividly into Luke 10:19 "Behold, I give you power to trend on serpents and scorpions, and over all the power of the enemy; and nothing shall by any means hurt you"*

From the scriptures above, He has power to destroy the works of the enemies; the same power was what He also gave to us that we may also take dominion over darkness. As children of God, we are expected to work with the consciousness that whatever it is God can do I can also do. This was the revelation Apostle Paul got when he said "I can do all things through Christ who strengthens me"-Philippians 4:13.

To cap it up, for a better understanding, let's take a look at John *14:12 "Verily verily. I say unto you, he that believes in me, the works that I do shall he do also, and greater works that these shall he do; because I go unto my father".* The conclusion of the matter now is whatever it is

Jesus did, you can also do. You are in the same image and likeness with Christ. In other words, the same making comprises your set up. If he enjoyed divine healing, you can also enjoy divine healing, if he has authority, you also have authority. Start making your research to see what it is that Christ has, I can always tell you to check on your inside, you have the same thing. The nature of God is embedded in His spirit. And since you carry the Holy Spirit you also carry the nature of God.

Third Principle:

God created man. This word 'MAN' that is used in this statement does not refer to gender as in male but rather a name that God gave to the spirit that came out of His Spirit. It is a Hebrew word "ISH" which means 'spirit", so it is essential to know that spirits have no gender and therefore mankind is neither male nor female, a pure spirit that came out of God. What makes a car is the engine not the body, what makes a church is the congregation not the structure, what makes a phone is the panel not the casing. In other words, what makes a man is the Spirit not the body.

Every other thing is just mere subordinate and ephemeral. Man is first addressed as a spirit, because it takes spirit to relate with spirit. God is a spirit and he could relate with Adam because man at first before his fall was more of spirit than flesh.

Fourth Principle:

God said let "them" have dominion over the earth. This statement is the most critical statement concerning mankind because it contains the most powerful secret to the transfer of power and authority from God Himself to mankind, from Heaven to earth. This is the fundamental divine delegation of responsibility for management and rulership of the earth to mankind. It is the most powerful delegation from God Himself that cannot be changed by anybody including God Himself, because the nature of God's holiness and integrity does not permit Him to violate His own words, and we see this in book of Psalm 138:2 which says, "For you have magnified your word above your name"; according to Hebrew custom the "name" of someone refers to his reputation and authority.

For that reason, God exalted His own

authority above all other things that are under His authority, even His authority itself. Moreover, whatever He speaks has to be established for Him to keep His reputation in line with His words or otherwise He will not be supreme; this is why we can trust God alone. Therefore, when God spoke these words, He established the conditions of His relationship to earth through mankind. He did not say let "US" have dominion over the earth, as that would have given Him legitimate access to earth without mention of mankind but rather "THEM". By these words, He established mankind as the only legal authority on earth, with the power of attorney to act on His behalf on earth. This is probably one of the reasons why God has never done anything on the earth without the cooperation of human entity and was ultimately the reason for the requirement of His access into the human race as a Man.

Many of course believe that God is unlimited which is very true, but may I tell you that the only thing that limits God is His word. Forever the word of God is settled. Whatever it is God will do must be in the confine of His word. Therefore, when the word says "let them have dominion", it means exactly what He said with the exception of none, not even God himself. This powerful declarative pronouncement was what gave humanity the super control and legal rule over the earth. Not even the devil has legal access to the earth but man.

It is the possession of spirit in the body of man that makes them manifest and interrupt the affairs of human on earth. Therefore, if any spirit being must have full operation on the planet earth, there must be a body as the host.

Jesus – the Man – made Christ – the God – legal on earth. This is the secret power mankind has on planet earth concerning his ultimate purpose.

Fifth Principle:

Let them have dominion. This statement in the Bible is a significant principle for understanding the nature and the desires of mankind. It expresses clearly the ultimate reason why God created mankind and was to have dominion over planet earth. This statement leaves us with no doubt of what motivated God to create mankind and His expectations concerning them.

It also establishes mankind's assignment and a measure of success for his existence. (Psalm 8:4, 9)

"What is mankind that you are mindful of them, human beings that you care for them, you have made them a little lower than the angels and crowned them with glory and honour. You made them rulers over the works of your hands; you put everything under their feet, all flocks and herds, and the animals of the wild, the birds in the sky, and the fish in the sea, all that swim the paths of the seas. Lord, our Lord, how majestic is your name in all the earth!" Add scripture. Psalm 8:4-9.

What a powerful and an amazing statement concerning the purpose of mankind. Only if all of us can capture and understand the purpose of God for creating mankind; Imagine how the world would be if we all discovered the purpose of existence of our purpose and ruled the world.

The dominion God gave man wasn't just with vague intention but a conspicuous awakening to what has been installed in the human system. Everything a man needs to come to the fullness of God is on the inside of the man, which is the Holy Spirit.

More so, God saying let them have dominion

implies that, human should come to the identity and have a knowledge of their position on earth. In other words, God is saying to man, you are not the same as the animals, not the same as the trees, not the same as the firmament, not the same as the crops and fruit but as God. Hence, dominion is an integral part of God's nature, which is also in man. "Let them have" is an active and authoritative statement. It wasn't a plea; neither was it a persuasion but a command.

Get the picture very well, God didn't say we should take care of the earth, He didn't say we should help keep the earth but He said have dominion. God did lay emphasis on the need for dominion. Four different components of dominion were revealed to us in Genesis 1:28 "And God blessed them, and God said unto them, be **fruitful** and **multiply** and **replenish** the earth, and **subdue** it; and have dominion over the fish of the sea, and over the fowls of the air, and over every living thing that moves upon the earth".

The first component of dominion is Fruitfulness means to be productive. The second component of dominion is Multiplication, which means to make something increase very much in number. The third is Replenish, which implies making something full again by replacing it with what has been used. The last component is Subdue, which connotes; to suppress something. That is, bringing something under control, especially by using force.

Corroboratively, having dominion entails fruitfulness, multiplication, replenishment and to subdue. In simple terms, it is the ability to be produce, make into larger number what you have produced, maintain the increase in production and the defeat of taking full control over anything that might want to go against or contrary to your production. This is the full package of dominion as ordered by God. The scope of man's dominion is a way of saying man is a manager. God has given man things under his custody to manage.

Sixth Principle:

Over the fish of the sea, birds of the air, the livestock, earth, and all that creeps upon the earth. This statement is crucial as it defines the nature and boundaries of the rulership of mankind; it gives specific details of what mankind should be ruling over. It is important to note that the human entity is not included in the delegation of mankind's domination. It is never God's intent for mankind to rule over or dominate his own kind (humans) but rather to rule over and dominate the creation and the resources of earth that have been given to his management.

God never intended for mankind to dominate another human but rather earth. God is not an author of confusion. He hasn't made any super human to overpower the other. Instead, he has relayed to us the sphere of our rulership and the capacity of our dominance.

Based on the scriptures and my understanding on the measure and sphere of our dominance, I know there are some prayers mean present that God will not answer, because our God is not a pioneer of confusion. Can you imagine a man of God threatening another man of God with the power of the Holy Ghost? It won't work. Can you comprehend a believer, praying for the downfall of another believer in other to show he has more relationship with God? It can't work, because the kingdom of light is a highly organised system. It is only in the world and in the kingdom of darkness that you can see an herbalist fighting against another herbalist with powers from the same spirit and one defeating the other or sometimes both herbalists suffer loss.

CHAPTER 4

WHAT IS DOMINION?

First of all, it is critical to understand and discover what God actually preordained when He made this incredible delegation concerning mankind, when He said, "let them "HAVE DOMINION" over the earth." I believe to completely grasp all the intentions of God concerning this delegation; we are first obligated to rediscover the actual meaning of word "dominion" because it has to do with the purpose of mankind.

According to the Oxford dictionary:

1. The power or right of governing and controlling; sovereign authority.

2. Rule; control; domination.

3. A territory, usually of considerable size, in which a single rulership holds sway.

4. Lands or domains subject to sovereignty or control.

5. Government.

Therefore, this definition of the word "dominion" according to the dictionary reveals to us the complete original purpose or intent of God concerning His species, mankind. That He created us to have complete, "Government," "sovereign authority," "control," "rulership," "management," "master," and lead the earth for Him as His representatives on the planet earth.

The original Hebrew translation of the word "dominion" is the word "mamlakah" or "malkut," in the original Greek it is the word "basileia." The definition of these words consists of "Kingship", "sovereignty," "authority," "to rule", "kingdom," "to reign," "to master," "to be king," "kingly," and "royal rule." The word "basileia" which also means "kingdom" is relentlessly used in relationship with the governing of Jesus Christ the Lord in the hearts of mankind.

Therefore, the definition of "dominion" can be crafted in the following way:

To be given "dominion" means to be established as a sovereign authority, kingly ruler, master, governor, and leader, accountable for reigning over a chosen territory. [12] So God's original purpose or intent concerning mankind is not hidden but rather revealed in the bible that we avoid reading and meditating. According to the bible mankind was created to be in "charge" over the territory "earth" that was chosen for him before the foundation of the earth. That he may rule as God's own personal ambassador to administer the kingdom of heaven on the planet earth.

The following scripture helps us to have a greater understanding of our dominion:

- 2 Corinthians 5:20, 'so we are Christ's ambassadors, God is making His appeal through us. We speak for Christ when we plead, "Come back to God'

- Matthew 6:10, 'Let your kingdom come,

---

[12] Psalm 115:16, "the highest heavens belong to the LORD, but the earth he has given to mankind."

your will be done, on earth as it is in heaven.'

HEAVEN ON EARTH

One of the conditions that the church of God has faced over the decades is that it has reversed the purpose of God for mankind; it has preoccupied people with leaving the earth rather than to have dominion over the earth as God intended. To such a degree our minds are set on the mission of going to Heaven rather a commission of Jesus Christ to occupy the earth until He comes. Several persons have come to conclude that heaven is their only goal and the reason why they are on earth. God has not created us to live a useless life on earth. He said, be fruitful and multiply on earth not in heaven. We need to know that God frowns at unproductive life. When Jesus and his disciples got to the tree and found no fruit, immediately, Jesus cursed the tree and it withered off. Also, Bible records it in the parable of the talent that the one that went to bury his talent was banished from the sight of the master, but the ones who multiplied theirs were appreciated. The master collected the talent of the unprofitable servant and gave it to those who have already. Hence, a deep clue and hint on God's mind towards living the earth without emptying your potentials here on earth. Everyman on earth has been designed by God to render a service, thus the reason why ministers are addressed as servant because they render a service.

The world is desolate because people who God originally intended to rule planet earth are quick to leave the very place that was created just for them to have rulership over everything illegal in the territory of the earth. Things such as pains, disease, brokenness, poverty, lack of peace and much more we think of.

Moreover, it is paramount to grasp that mankind was not created for Heaven but rather for the earth. The territory that was chosen for him by God himself to rule as an administrator of God to transfer His heavenly kingdom on earth through mankind so that earth may look like heaven as God intended it to be from the beginning in the Garden of Eden. In the Garden of Eden, there was nothing such as pains, poverty, brokenness, disease, lack of peace and much more, but rather a complete wholeness in the presence of God Almighty, the Creator of all things through relationship.

Heaven is not our home but earth is. It is the place God made for mankind to rule over. So the right response to injustice and brokenness is to engage the struggle to overcome it, not to leave it.

Seeing the Bible as a Heaven-promising book blinds us to biblical truth about a renewed creation. The Bible's description of the destination of the mankind is never "heaven," but rather "earth" and the resurrection of the dead, the renewal of all things, and the time for God to restore everything, the liberation of creation, the new heavens and the new earth, and the life of the age to come. This is the original intent of God concerning mankind.[13]

The following scriptures can also be used to offer greater clarity in respect of mankind moving on to heaven:

▪ Revelation 21:1, 'Then I saw "a new heaven and a new earth," for the first heaven and the first earth had passed away, and there was no longer any sea.'

---

[13] Isaiah 26:19, Daniel 12:2, Mathew 22:30

- Isaiah 65:17, 'For behold, I create new heavens and a new earth: and the former shall not be remembered, nor come into mind.'

Based on the biblical description, Heaven appears to be both a place and a state. But more than that, it is best described as the realm in which God himself rules, whilst earth is where you and I rule as God's ambassadors. This explains Jesus' prayer that, 'God's will be done on earth as it is in heaven.' He is saying, "Let your kingdom rulership come to us as it is with you right now in your glorious Heaven." Jesus never demanded God to take us to heaven but rather to keep us here on earth, that the heavenly rulership authority of God might also be transfer here on earth through mankind, that the earth may know how heaven is like.

John 17:15: "My prayer is not that you take them out of the world but that you protect them from the evil one". This is suggesting Mankind is simply created to rule the earth for GOD, but not heaven. God never gave man dominion over heaven but rather over earth God never promised mankind heaven but rather earth.

Heaven seems to be a place where we live

before returning to earth with Jesus for the second coming, but our ultimate hope is that heaven and earth will be united and rule as they did in the garden of Eden. Heaven is a waiting room for the second coming of Jesus and the new heavens and a new earth, just as hell is a waiting room for the lake of fire.

In Eden, the realms of heaven and earth were together as one. God walked with mankind. However, when sin entered the world, these realms were separated. In the book of Revelation 21 and 22, it gives a great detail concerning the purpose of God for mankind after death, that these realms come back together as God intended. It is interesting that in the book of "Revelation" we don't go "up" to heaven, but rather a new earth and new heavens come "down" to us.

Ephesians 1:10, 'and this is the plan: At the right time he will bring everything together under the authority of Christ-everything in heaven and on earth.'

Revelation 5:10, "you have made them to be a kingdom (sovereign) authority and priests (spiritual administrators) to serve our God, and they will reign on the earth."

God's original intent for mankind was, still is and will always be for mankind to administer His kingdom rulership over the earth rather the earth to heaven. God has already made an arrangement for mankind that he will not stay in Heaven but rather come back to his original territory earth that was specifically created for him by God Himself to dominate as God's ambassadors.

Hoping for Heaven distracts us from our fundamental human purpose. From start to finish, the Bible is inviting us into a certain way of being in the world. To be made in the image of God is to reflect God's character and intention in the way we shape life on earth. To such a degree heaven is not our ultimate destination but rather earth is, as God originally intended for us to have king dominion over the earth. To dominate the planet as He intended since the creation of the earth and God will always get what He originally wanted, (Proverbs 19:21) that is His Heavenly Kingdom on earth through mankind. It is also very important to define the meaning of word "KINGDOM" since is attached to mankind's original purpose.

CHAPTER 5

WHAT IS A KINGDOM?

A kingdom is simply the territory of a King, extending His sovereign rulership authority over another territory that is manifested through the citizens that he chose to be His administrator representatives over that territory. So it's called KING-DOM

KING: Ruler

DOM: Dominion, domain, territory, realm

So mankind is the 'King', which God intended to use to transfer His heavenly kingdom rulership authority on earth.

Heaven: invisible – God's territory

Earth: visible – Mankind's territory

As aforementioned the very plans and purpose of God were, still and will always be simply to transfer His heavenly kingdom rulership authority over the earth through the people who He calls His own "SONS", that is mankind Psalm 82:6 " ", John 1:12, 1John 3:2. But when the very people that God intended to use to transfer His heavenly kingdom on earth, "REBELLED" against Him, they were automatically disconnected from God and from the very delegation of kingdom rulership authority (dominion) that was conferred on them by God Himself.

Adam was disqualified from representing the kingdom of God on earth because you cannot represent a country that you are not connected with. Henceforth, it is important to understand that the first man, Adam, lost the very connection of the government that he was meant to represent as an ambassador on earth.

Genesis 2:17, 'but of the tree of the knowledge of good and evil you shall not eat, for in the day that you eat of it you shall surely die.'

This death was not referring primarily to physical death; though that would be the ultimate result, but rather to mankind's spiritual disconnection from His very source God and the kingdom authority. This is evidenced by the fact that Adam lived 930 years after the act of disobedience against God. Therefore, death to God was disconnection and independence (self-government) from God and the kingdom of Heaven. Adam lost the kingdom (sovereign authority) over the earth. The consequences of this rebellion were numerous:

1. Loss of position and disposition

Adam lost his position in the presence of God. He couldn't relate with God as it used to be before. Things changed suddenly and he could not stand where he usually meets with God. He needed to go and hid himself.

What exactly was the position he lost? The position in the real sense was his relationship with God. The bible tells us that God comes to visit Adam in the cool of the evening. In other words, they talk, commune and relate as father to son. Of course, many said he lost his position in the Garden of Eden, that's true but much more you need to understand deeply that Eden is not just a place but also the presence of God.

Eden is the meeting place between God and Adam. So categorically, Eden is the abode of God on earth. It is a place of fellowship, it is a place where the visible presence of God can be seen, and it is a place that is most comfortable and suitable for mankind. These all were what Adam lost. Little wonder why he could not see God but only hear his voice after the fall. Adam lost his position in the presence of God

Adam lost his disposition. Adam before the fall was a spiritual man, because it takes spirit to relate with spirit. God doesn't relate with flesh but spirit. Bible says in *John 4:24 "God is a Spirit and they that must worship Him must worship Him in sprit and in truth"'* **(KJV)** In other words, Adam lost this spiritual ability. His spiritual eyes became blind and his fleshly eyes became open and the scriptures say 'Their eyes were opened and they saw that they were both naked...' It was also after they have eaten the forbidden fruit that they knew that there was good and evil. All they knew before was just the mind and the will of God. God told them when you eat of the fruit at the centre of the garden you will surely die, but the devil deceived that they won't die.

In the long run they ate the fruit and they were expecting death just has God has told them but they didn't die a physical death as expected, unknown to them that it was more of a spiritual death than a physical one. Several people commit sin or go contrary to God's will and they are expecting one strange and evil thing to happen instantly to them and they discovered nothing happened. They conclude in their heart that nothing eventually happened. This is a deception from the pit of hell, when you continue in sin, something happens in the spirit but you might not know it so soon. The scripture says in Romans 6:1 'What shall we say then? Shall we continue in sin that grace may abound?' God forbid.

2. Transfer of responsibility

Responsibility in my simple term is coined out from two words namely; "RESPONSE" and "ABILTY". The combination of these two words gives us "RESPONSIBILITY". Simply put, responsibility means responding to your ability (potentials).

God gave Adam several abilities. It was Adam that gave names to the plants, he also gave names to animals, and whatsoever Adam called it that was what it is.

Adam's responsibility of keeping the garden was taken away from him. The responsibility of taking charge of the garden, the animals and all other things was lost. Unlike before that he will give account to God of how he kept the garden, he no longer has any work or God given assignment to do again. Adam was out of God's presence; therefore, he couldn't control the animals the way he used to do. When a man leaves God's presence, he no longer carries the capacity to do God's work efficiently, because doing God's assignment involves constant carrying of God's presence. The scriptures say 'without me, you can do nothing'. Whenever a man disconnects himself from the source, he will not get resources in times of need. Whenever a man disconnects himself from the father (GOD), he cannot go farther. When Adam got disconnected from God, he became jobless, he became stranded and miserable; the purpose was which he was created was thwarted.

3. Self-consciousness and shame

Adam, as soon as he ate the fruit; the bible says that 'And their eyes were both opened and they knew that they were naked'. The word knew as used in the scripture above means they came to the self-consciousness of themselves, their eyes were opened to see their natural state. They discovered they don't look like God again, little wonder they hid themselves. Before now, they have been spirit-conscious, they have always seen themselves in resemblance of character, nature and deed like God but as soon as they fell, the nature of God in them changed and the saw their physical nature instead of the spiritual nature.

There is no nakedness in the spirit, neither is there difference in dress in the spirit. Spirits don't wear clothes. It was after they fell they began to make leaves to cover themselves. That's why the spiritual man doesn't bother on things of this world because they don't count to him. Spirit doesn't drive cars. Desires of this world started when man fell at the beginning.

Shame came to them in the garden. Before the fall of man there was nothing to be ashamed of, because there's nothing like shame with God.

When God placed them in the garden they didn't know what shame was. Shame exists because man fell. They saw that they were naked and became ashamed. One of the things sin has brought to humanity is shame.

When a man suddenly discovers that the shield or attire covering him falls off and his nakedness appears to people, what happens? He becomes ashamed. What then has been covering the nakedness of man before the fall? I discovered that the glory of God has been the covering over them in the garden but as soon as they disobeyed God by eating the forbidden fruit, the glory which was a cover upon them was taken away. At that point, they discovered they were naked.

When a man commits sin, it can make the glory of God disappear from him. What then is the definition of nakedness? A man is said to be spiritually naked when the grace and glory of God covering him is taken away. The bible says and the name of the child was called Ichabod for the glory is taken away from Israel. It was the sin that brought shame into existence.

4. Fear and intimidation of authority

Fear was also one of the consequences that accompanied the fall of man. After Adam ate the fruit, God called him and he was afraid to appear before God. *Genesis 3:10 "And he said I heard thy voice in the garden and I was afraid, because I was naked and I hid myself." (KJV)* whenever a man transgresses a law or breaks a rule, what pops up in his heart is fear. What type of fear? Fear of the unknown, fear of consequences, fear of punishment, fear of result of what has been done wrongly, and fear of danger, etc. When you look at the kinds of fear I highlighted above, you will see that it was all based on a sort of bounce-back, or a sort of result birthed from what has been done. When something has been wrongly done, Fear sets in. Fear most times comes from the product of what has been done in the past. In other words, when God called Adam, he was so afraid, because he knew he has disobeyed the instructions of God. The reason he was not fearful before was because he was in right standing with God, but as soon as he disobeyed fear sets in.

Fear has for a long time been the tool of the devil to scare people away from God. The devil makes people believe running far from God is the best way to escape the wrath of God. Therefore, he has captivated so many people into believing that God cannot forgive them because of the extent of their sin which is a blatant lie. *Hebrews 4:16 "let us therefore come boldly unto the throne of grace that we may obtain mercy and find grace to help in times of need"* See in the scriptures how we are asked to react to the father whenever we sin. We are to come boldly to the throne for mercy, though not with smiling and triviality but with a sense of soberness and remorsefulness.

The key point there is; don't allow the devil to keep deceiving you that God cannot forgive you. This what the trick the devil instilled in the heart of Adam, that made fear grip him

The authority of Adam was intimidated. Adam has been the one in charge of everything in the garden and suddenly because of sin he was in charge of nothing. Wild animals were not supposed to scare or harm human because God already gave us authority over them, but contrary to these, animals had such a great enmity for human. Several creatures that give obeisance Adam no longer do such.

5. The loss of domination over nature

Dominion over other creatures became a thing of the past for Adam. He was no longer in control. He tried controlling things and instructing them the way he used to but they weren't responding at all, because the glory and presence of God they saw before was what makes them obey him. He lost his leadership and power over nature. What exactly was the scope of dominion of man in the first place? Scriptures reveals to us in *Genesis 1:28-30 "28. And God blessed them, and God said unto them, be fruitful and multiply, and replenish the earth, and subdue it; and have dominion over the fish of the sea and the fowl of the air, and over 29. And God said, behold I have given you every herb bearing seed, which is upon the face of all the earth, and every tree of a fruit yielding seed; to you it shall be for meat. 30. and to every beast of the earth and to every fowl of the air, and to everything that crept upon the earth, where in there is life, I have given every green seed for meat and it was so".*

This was the dominion given to man by God over all he has made; both living and non-living but sin took all these away at a glance. What a severe consequence for rebellion.

6. Frustration toil and hatred of labour

Another consequence of the fall of man was toil and hard labour. Man in its original state was not designed by God to engage in stress and hard labour. As a matter of fact, things happen at ease, but after the fall, man began to till the ground before he can eat. Man had to labour before he could feed. Genesis 3:17b 'cursed is the ground for thy sake, in sorrow shall thou eat all the days of thy life'. The above scripture was the foundation of struggle, labour and frustration in mankind. That is why if you see globally today there is labour and struggle for people who will rise. After the eating of the fruit, Adam's life was heavily frustrated and toilsome. Life became so hard. For the very first time Adam believed hard labour is the surest way if he must survive and feed well, unlike before when he eats fruits and meat freely without any stress or work so to say. Labour was not in God's plan for humanity in the beginning. The labour women pass through during child bearing is a result of the consequence of the fall of man. The delivery of a child could have been as easy and smooth as whatever you can think of. Just imagine the labour they go through just to put a child to bed. What a devastating change.

7. Pain and discomfort

The structure and functions of the body in the beginning does not permit pain. In the beginning the operation and exhibition of man was more of spiritual than physical. Spirit doesn't feel pain. Therefore, Adam being a spiritual man when his ways was right with God did not have pain, until the fall. Adam never mentioned any pain at all, until the fall; that child bearing becomes painful and tough. The scriptures say Genesis 3:16 'Unto the woman, i will greatly multiply thy sorrows and conception; in sorrow thou shall bring forth children...'Even till date bringing forth children has been highly excruciating. Sorrow has been the order of the day, just because man fell.

Comfort a language so far from men. Permit to say what we have in the beginning is called ready-made, because God had put things in place for Adam. He just had the responsibility to keep it. There was No need for planting seed, there was no need for tilling the ground, and there was no need for preserving because of spoilage or decay of foods. Never! Everything thing in the beginning was already made by God. Another picture of such already-made food was what the Israelites enjoyed in the wilderness by feeding on manna for forty years. Now it is no longer like that.

8. The need for human accountability and many more

An inevitable consequence of the fall of man was what man became accountable, that is, man was responsible for every actions taken and must be ready to explain why the decisions were taken. Before now, God was responsible for anything needed in the Garden of Eden, He was also responsible for the provision of man, but at the fall of man, man became responsible for food, work, labour, and many others.

Mankind did not lose Heaven but rather earth and dominion authority over earth.

THE DOMINION OF AUTHORITY

To understand the loss of dominion and assignment over the earth is crucial to first realise you cannot lose what you have never had. Adam the first representative of God's kingdom on earth was entrusted with the responsibility of serving as Heaven's earthly ambassador. But it's important to know that an ambassadorial representative is only as valid and legal as his relationship with his government.

When an ambassador is disconnected from the very government that he was meant to represent, he is no longer a legal representative of that government but rather illegitimate. Therefore, the most important relationship the first man, Adam, had on earth was with heaven. This is why the HOLY SPIRIT of God was intimate with mankind from the very beginning of His creation. His dwelling presence guaranteed constant communication and fellowship with the will, mind, intent and purpose of God and heaven so that He could execute His governments will on earth. As a matter of fact, any VISION that doesn't start with the Holy Spirit will end in DIVISION. Man cannot afford to do anything without the leading of the Holy Spirit. This Spirit is the channel through which God reaches mankind. God does not relate to our bodies neither does he relates with our mind but He reaches out to us through the spirit. The Holy Spirit is the seal of promise upon every child of God. What guarantees and certifies our being as a child of God is the possession of the Holy Spirit. The following scriptures give an illuminating comprehension to the essentiality of the Holy Spirit.

Romans 8:14 'For as many as are led by the Spirit of God, they are the sons of God'

Romans 8:16 says, 'The Spirit itself bears witness with our spirit that we are the children of God'.

Luke 4:18 'The spirit of the lord is upon me, because he has anointed me to preach the gospel to the poor, he has sent me to heal the broken hearted, to preach deliverance to the captives and recovering of sight to the blind, to set at liberty them that are bruised'.

In addition, relationship with the Holy Spirit is keen, if man must tread the path of greatness and success on earth. In a world like this, it is clear and visible that the spiritual controls the physical. It is moreover an apt decision to be at the controlling end which is the spiritual end.

This relationship makes the Holy Spirit of God the most important person on earth and established Him as the key component of the kingdom of heaven on earth. The loss or separation of mankind from the Holy Spirit of God would render mankind a disqualified representative of Heaven on earth, for mankind would not know the will or mind of the government of heaven for earth.

This is why the first encounter of mankind with the adversary, the devil in the book of Genesis chapter 3 was to attack the very relationship that mankind had in the Garden of Eden with God. Consequently, mankind has lost the kingdom rulership of heaven on earth.

"Mankind lost the relationship with God and instead gained religion." "God never intended for mankind to have religion but instead an effective relationship with Him."

THE GREATEST CRIME

The greatest crime committed in any kingdom or nation is the crime of treason. As a matter of fact, the death penalty is still the punishment for treason in some countries, whilst it is imprisonment in others.

It is the ultimate act of betrayal. Treason, therefore, is the crime that is the most serious act of betrayal of one's sovereign nation. Thus, you will ultimately have to be put to death or be imprisoned. Let us now define the word treason since is the highest act of betrayal against a government. According to Oran's Dictionary of the Law (1983) "TREASON" is defined as a citizen's actions to help a foreign government overthrow, make war against, or seriously injure the parent nation.

God gave Adam and Eve the greatest form of trust possible by giving them the dominion authority to rule as kings upon the earth to represent Him. It was one of the highest honours that God gave them. Nevertheless, the fall of man in the Garden of Eden disrupted the programme of God as they disobeyed His commandment. Therefore, the fall of man was not just an act of disobedience but rather of treason. Adam and Eve surrendered their dominion ruling authority over the earth to Satan and now he has the legal right to rule the earth; it was the ultimate act of betrayal, deserving the penalty of death immediately. Adam gave the keys of this kingdom to the devil. Adam who has been the one in charge of the earth lost his authority and power all of a sudden due to sin. Unknowing to him, he handed over his power and dominion over the earth.

When the bible described the devil as father of liars, it is a real truth. The only thing the devil told man was that he would be like God and know the difference between good and bad. This seems a bit cool to hearing, but he never told Adam that his rule and dominion will be taken away, he never told him that his throne of rulership would be transferred from him, he never told him that he would lose his connection with the father, he never told Adam that his tenure of being God's ambassador will expire, he never told him that it would lead to pain, frustration and death, he never told them they would die spiritually, he never told them they would cause a great harm to humanity. In other words, there were several things devil knew would be the consequence of the sin but he never mentioned that to them. That's to show how tricky and deceitful the devil can appear most times. That's to tell you that for every good you think the devil has for man, there are stocks of evil set to follow the good. It wasn't a mere say that the scriptures quote "There is a way that seems good to man, but the end thereof is the way of death (destruction)". The scripture also says "it is the lord that makes rich and added no sorrow to it" whatever it is that the devil presents good and nice on the outside, is totally bad on the inside".

The devil has made up his mind, since he lost his stand and place in heaven, he must dominate here on earth. Even before the fall of the devil, what he fought for was the throne of God. He wants to rule, he wants to dominate, he wants to displace God, he wants to be in charge too, he wants to exercise authority over all, and he also doesn't want anyone to direct him. He therefore made a conspiracy and plot to over throne God. What he couldn't achieve in heaven was what he came to achieve on earth. He had always wanted to rule, having seen the beauty and authority of being in charge. That is why the devil has been the greatest interruption we have here on earth.

The earth was now condemned to be ruled by the viciousness, cruelty, corruptness and oppression of Satan and his agents. As a result of that, Adam declared independence from his kingdom government, the kingdom of Heaven, abandoned his position as ambassador and lost his dominion rulership over the earth. Through the transaction of his responsibility as King over the earth, Adam lost the most important relationship of all, the HOLY SPIRIT of God. Through the violation of God's word, mankind was rendered a disqualified representative of the kingdom of Heaven on earth. God's agenda for man was placed on hold. Man could not further express the fullness of purpose. The capacity to exhibit God's nature ceased from man. Man was no longer in responsible and relevant in service to God. No one could represent God on earth. The mind of God for humanity was truncated and God was in search of someone who will stand out again to continue the mandate.

As soon as the government (authority) were transferred to the devil, pain, suffering, anguish, confusion, crisis, violence, hatred and destruction came to the human race. The system of the world changed, for the first time, the earth knew famine, the earth knew hardship, the earth knew tilling of the soil, knew suffering, and knew no peace. All these happened at the fall of man.

When Adam fell through this act of treason, he did not only lose his personal relationship with his heavenly Father but he also lost a kingdom, sovereign-ruling authority over the earth. Adam became a king without a kingdom and a ruler without a domain. Still, you may ask the same questions that I used to ask myself, why did God not dispose of the devil in that very moment, if He has the power to do it? Why has God permitted Satan to rule the earth and cause so much misery If He is God Almighty? I ultimately believe the answer to these questions lies only in God's word itself. First of all, we need to understand that God is righteous and perfectly just in all of His doing.

He does not overstep the legal bounds of freedom of will and dominion that He originally established with Adam and Eve in the Garden of Eden. Adam was given the legal right by God Himself to rule the earth, and therefore the freedom to transfer this right to whomsoever he chooses. When Adam chose to transfer this legal right to the devil, if God had come down and immediately destroyed the devil in the Garden of Eden and repossessed this legal right, it would have been an act of lawlessness.

God would have broken His own word and as a result of that, we wouldn't be able to trust Him. But since God is the God of His word, He made a promise to Satan in that very moment according to Genesis 3:14-15. Stating that, He would bring to an end the dominion that Adam gave to him over the earth and completely destroy him in the future, according to His perfect justice and righteous nature. However, he had no choice but to recognise the legal authority that the devil had been given by Adam. God is bound by His nature and His word, even to respect His enemy's legal rights.

The devil has legally obtained the authority and dominion to rule the earth. It could not be legally revoked or even declared void. It could not be cancelled or overruled. It was a terrible act of high treason and rebellion by Adam and Eve, and it gave the devil the legal authority and right to ruin God's creation. The earth has a new ruler, and he is wicked, cruel filled with hatred and bitterness. He is the enemy of God. He has decided to attack the creatures of God, especially human, and indeed there has been a great deal of war from the devil to humanity because of the shame of him losing his rights and position while in heaven.

THE PROMISE

It is very important to note, right after Adam and Eve surrendered their dominion ruling authority over the earth to Satan, which is known as the "fall of man', God immediately made a promise to Satan, found in Genesis 3:15 directly to His enemy, Satan: "And I will cause enmity between you and the woman, and between your seed and her seed. He will strike your head, and you will strike His heel."

This passage of scripture shows the first pronouncement or prophecy of the Messiah that He would be born through the seed of a young woman. Not only is this a prophecy of His birth but also it is a prophecy of His work. This is what He meant by "the seed of the woman", that sometime during the course of world history there would be an outstanding Man Child Redeemer, born of woman into the world. God said to Satan, "That Man Child Redeemer will crush your head."

Now, it is very critical to discover and to understand the symbolic meaning of the word "HEAD" in the original context of the word used in this particular scripture where God describes how He would defeat Satan and take the dominion authority and give it back to mankind, which was legally handed to Satan by Adam and Eve.

The original word used in this verse is the word "archōn" which is translated as "ruler", "prince", "leader", "power," "leading man," and "governor." God originally gave this right to Adam and Eve over the planet earth. However, when they disobeyed and went against God's word and chose to listen to the voice of the enemy by eating the fruit that God originally told them not to eat, the authority over the planet earth was instantly legally transferred to Satan. He then became the ruler, prince, power, leader, leading man and governor over the earth in that very moment. More so, the bible consequently, addressed the devil as the prince of this world, because he now operates in the office where Adam was supposed to occupy. This was what dominion the devil eyed, thereby luring man to fall which he achieved.

So, therefore, it is important to understand that for God to take back legal authority that He gave to mankind over the earth He had to make a legal guarantee to Satan that He would come on the earth as a Man through the seed of a virgin. "The purpose of Jesus Christ was for a re-connection of authority on earth to mankind, not to take them to Heaven."The reason for God coming to the earth in flesh was to present him rightful to exhibit His plans on earth. God could not interfere into the earth because it was out of the scope of His words to do so, and God will never contradict his word. Though, He devised a means of coming to the earth and that's why we have Jesus.

CHAPTER 6

RECONNECTION OF DOMINION AUTHORITY

Hence it is crucial to understand the purpose of the coming of the Messiah Jesus Christ our Lord on the planet earth and His work, was not to take mankind back to Heaven because that's not where mankind fell from, but instead, to reconnect them to their place of dominion authority over the earth where God originally intended for them to be.

Many have been so cautious of heaven –which is a good one-but at the detriment of their reign on earth, which makes it wrong. Many will say, now that I am saved let me remain this way and make heaven. Haba! There's more to being a child of God than just being saved only to go to heaven while we neglect our place on earth. God has laid several emphases enough in His word to portray his desire for humanity to dominate this earth. I think by now we should have a concrete and a profound understanding that our assignments is more of earth than in heaven.

The following scriptures confirm the mind of God towards the dominion of man on the surface of the earth.

Matthew 5:13, 14&16, "13. Ye are the salt of the earth; but if the salt lose its savour, wherewith shall it be salted again? It is thenceforth god for nothing, but to be cast out and trodden under the foot of men... 14. Ye are the light of the world. A city that is set on a hill cannot be hidden... 16. Let your light so shine before men that they may see your good works and glorify your father which is in heaven".

From the above scripture we can glaringly and obviously see that it is the mind of God that mankind takes rulership of this earth and explore it to the fullest. The scriptures say 'you are the salt of the earth', not the salt of heaven. It further says 'you are the light of the world' not the light of heaven. Should it not occur to you now that your essence as human is to manifest the kingdom of God in heaven here on earth? Salt makes things sweet. It stands for sweetness.

The question is; is the world sweet? Is the world indeed a safe place? Is the world peaceful? Of course your answer should be "NO" considering what we are experiencing today. And it's all because the so called children of God have refused to recognise their essence and imperative importance on earth, thereby, realising the kingdom of earth just like Adam did in the beginning to the devil.

God says if the salt lost its favour (sweetness; the reason for which it was created), it is therefore good for nothing. How will God load us up with treasures and potentials and the best we can do with it is to keep it while we focus on heaven, seriously? God says if a man refuse to take charge on earth he is good for nothing.

Another dimension of our dominion on earth is that we are the light of the world, a city that is set on a hill that cannot be hidden. It's so pitiful that children of God are the ones covering their light from shining. As we know that light gives illumination and brightness and of course where light is darkness disappears. Light also clears off every form of confusion, chaos, and danger. That's why havoc is perpetrated more at night than the day time, why? The reason is not farfetched, in the presence of darkness, there will be no vision and where there's no vision people get into confusion which can lead to destruction. The earth was full of darkness and God has placed human on Earth to maintain and sustain the light here on earth.

Can you imagine someone fuelling your generating set in the day so that you won't feel the darkness at night, only for you to discover that by night, there is still darkness everywhere, and when you were asked what happened, you said; "Actually, I don't want the fuel to finish and I really want to maintain the generating set so that it doesn't have any fault". The fact remains why then do you have generating set in the first place? Why then was the generator fuelled? At that point you would say it is good for nothing, because it's not fulfilling the purpose it was made for.

Many believers are living their lives in this same mindset of the aforementioned illustration that heaven is my goal and anything on earth that may likely appear to stop me, I dump them, even including God's gift in them, the potentials and the light He embedded in them, and they dumped everything.

Reconciliation between man and God has been the plan of God for man. God has been looking for a way to bring humanity back into their initial glory and mandate. He has always desired that man comes back to rulership and place of authority so that His will and mandate for humanity will be a reality. Enough of the incessant dominion and cruel act of the devil over humanity, so the need for God to intervene. Since man could not help escape from the control of the devil, God need to show up to deliver humanity from the kingdom of darkness and translates us into the kingdom of His dear son. I'll like you to follow me through this scripture, to have a solid view and processes exhibited in God re-installing humanity back to his first seat of dominion and authority.

Colossians 1:13 "Who hath delivered us from the kingdom of darkness and has translated us into the kingdom of His dear son". Also let's see *Colossians 2:14-15 "14. Blotting out the handwriting of ordinances that was against us, which was contrary to us, and took it out of the way, nailing it to the cross. 15. Having spoiled principalities and powers, he made a show of them openly, triumphing over them in it". (KJV)*

These scriptures explicitly express the freedom of man from the bondage of the devil, from the rule of wickedness and from the yoke of sin. It gives us a limpid picture of our deliverance from the custody and administration of darkness. God didn't just deliver us but he brought us back, He reconciled us, He reinstated us.

First of all, he delivered us from the influence of the devil, removed the seal of slavery, took the debts of sin and its consequences and nailed them all to the cross. Thereafter, he spoiled (defeated) principalities and powers and made an open fun of them. All these were done just for God to re-ignite the fellowship and relationship that we enjoyed in the beginning.

The devil being completely ignorant of the strategy of God, coming through Jesus Christ, put up all efforts to abort his emergence into the planet earth. Herod tried killing Jesus but he failed, even though the death of several children went with it, yet Jesus was rescued from the plot of King Herod. When it became glaring that Jesus was the saviour, they conspired to kill him. Unknowingly, they were helping to fast track the plans of God. They never knew the death and resurrection of Jesus was what is needed to redeem man to his rightful source. They flogged him in several strokes not knowing that His stripes will be the medicine for our healing. Scripture says *1 Peter 2:24 "Who His own sin bears our iniquities on the tree, that we, being dead to sins, should live unto righteousness; by whose stripes ye are healed" (KJV)*

I literally believe with all my heart that to be an effective believer or representative on earth for God, we need to have some form of understanding of the purpose of Jesus Christ coming to earth and what He came to do. Growing up as a young believer who was just getting to know Jesus, I struggled with couple questions regarding the coming of Jesus on earth. Did He come to take us to Heaven, and then if that's the case why are we still here on this planet? Why can't God just take us straight away instead of waiting until the end of the world? I couldn't work my head around it until the Holy

Ghost spoke to me clearly. He stated the following "Son, the purpose of Jesus coming to earth was to reconnect mankind back into the Garden of Eden, where I put them with full authority over the earth through the HOLY SPIRIT."[14]

Accordingly, Spirit had to leave the body of man because it became contaminated with sin. The Holy Spirit is holy; He cannot dwell in a vessel that is contaminated but only in a vessel that is clean since His nature is holy. Now for a man to be reconnected back to his source of authority through the Holy Spirit his body must be cleansed so that the Holy Spirit may once again dwell inside of man. Only then will man regain his dominion over the earth as God intended. The Old Testament records that the Holy Spirit was only coming upon mankind in the form of visitation to accomplish a certain mission and then He would leave because mankind's body was yet to become cleansed.

Before now (the Old Testament), the Holy Spirit was addressed as "Spirit upon" but now (after the day of Pentecost), it became "Spirit within". Here are scriptures to solidify your

---

[14] Revelation 5:10, "And you have made them a kingdom and priests to our God, and they shall reign on the earth."

understanding on the dispensation of the Spirit upon and Spirit within.

- ## Spirit Upon

Judges 15:14 "And he came unto Lehi, the philistines shouted against him; and the Spirit of the lord CAMEMIGHTILY UPON him and the cords of that were upon his arms became as flax that was burnt with fire, and his bands loosed from off his hands".

Ezekiel 11:5 "And the Spirit of the lord FELL UPON me, speak; thus says the lord; thus have you said, o house of Israel; for I know the things that come into your mind, everyone of them".

Numbers 24:2, "And Balaam lifted up his eyes, and he saw Israel abiding in his tents according to their tribes, and the Spirit of the lord CAME UPON him". (KJV)

- ## Spirit Within

1Corinthians 3:16 "know ye not that ye are the temple of God, and the spirit of God which dwells in you".

2ndCorinthinas 6:16 "And what agreement has the temple of God with idols? For ye are the temple of the living God; as God has said, I will

DWELL IN THEM, and WALK IN THEM; and I will be their God, and they shall be my people". *(KJV)*

These and lot more of scriptures affirm the residence of the Holy Spirit in human in this present time.

How can we become holy that we may regain our authority again through Holy Spirit?

Hebrews 9:22 states the following, "In fact, the law requires that nearly everything is cleansed with blood, and without the shedding of blood there is no forgiveness." Thus, it must be noted that the cleansing of the body of mankind only required the blood of the Son of God, Jesus Christ, because only the blood of Jesus could cleanse our sin and remove the shame of our actions. This is why He had to die as the man Jesus. Jesus Christ was both 100 percent flesh and blood man and 100 percent divine Son of God. We cannot separate the two; to do so would be to deny the work that He did on the cross.

We cannot worship Christ and forget about Jesus because without Jesus we cannot have Christ. The blood of Jesus cleansed our sin and created the basis for our forgiveness, making it possible for Christ to restore us to righteousness and holiness. Bringing unto us the HOLY SPIRIT to live and abide in us that we may regain our dominion authority over the earth again.

There is no alternative way to it; it was the Holy Spirit that left man due to sin, that made man empty and subdued by the devil, if then we must take back our dominion, the Holy Spirit is an essential factor in living a spirit-filled and purposeful life. Wherever we find the Holy Spirit, there is peace, unity, love, harmony, joy, victory and so on.

Nevertheless, the Spirit functions in purity and not in filthiness. Although the blood of Jesus serves as remissions for our sins and also washes our sins away, yet we must come to the responsibility of taking up the step of presenting ourselves holy and acceptable. *Romans 12:1 "I beseech you therefore, brethren, by the mercies of God, that ye present your body a living sacrifice, Holy, acceptable unto God, which is your reasonable service"*

This shows that we have roles to play before the infilling of the Holy Spirit. Here are the sequential and vital roles to play for the Holy

Spirit to be resident in you.

First and foremost, you need to acknowledge (accepting and recognize) the lordship of Jesus Christ and believe that He is the Son of God. You must believe He died and resurrected the third day and ascended to heaven. When you accept (confess Him with your mouth) and believe Him with your heart, you get saved. *Romans 10:10 says "For with heart man believeth unto righteousness; but with mouth confession is made unto salvation". John 1:12 "But as many as received Him, to them gave He the power to become the sons of God", Mark 16:16 "He that believed and his baptized shall be saved, but he that believes not shall be damned".*

Additionally, when a man accepts and believes Jesus Christ, he is saved. By the way, may I tell you this; "If you are not SAVED, you are not SAFE". When a man is saved, he has the Holy Spirit residing in him. Howbeit, it's not enough for the Holy Spirit to be resident (at rest) but president (at work and in charge) in man.

The person of the Holy Spirit in man is non-negotiable and indispensable. Can you imagine a car without engine, though the car has good parts and tyres, who cares? Can you imagine a drink without its liquid content, though the container looks very beautiful and well designed, who cares? Can you imagine a phone without any panel, but have a nice casing, it still doesn't count right? In the same trend, can you imagine a life without the Holy Spirit? Miserable, purposeless, disoriented and limited, right Yes! You're correct. No matter the luxury of clothes, houses and fleet of cars a man has, if he doesn't have the Holy Spirit he's in danger. All others things can't give you the Holy Spirit but the Holy Spirit can give you all other things. *Matthew 6:33 "But seek ye first, the kingdom of God and His righteousness and all other things shall be added unto you."*

WHY THE BLOOD OF JESUS?

Only the blood of Jesus Christ was able to bring redemption and restoration to mankind. The Jewish law in the Old Testament required the blood sacrifices of animals; they were a constant visual reminder that the blood of an innocent victim was the price required to take away our sins. In this way, the Jewish sacrificial system anticipated or looked ahead to, the day when

Jesus, the Lamb of God, pure and sinless, would shed His blood. His blood was sufficient once and for all to cleanse us and to cover our sin.

It was and saliently obvious that the blood of rams, bulls, cows and other animals of sacrifice could no longer serve as propitiation for the sin of man, thus, the need for a special and unique blood; the blood of the Jesus. *Ephesians 1:7, "In whom we have redemption through His blood, the forgiveness of sins, according to the riches of His grace".* It can warmly be inferred that, the blood of Jesus is the channel through which everyone has redemption and also forgiveness of sin. Justification came to man through the blood of Jesus. The blood frees us from the guilt and the nature of sin. We become free from shame and the consequences of sin, because the blood paid the price. The blood erases the ugly past and gives us a fresh new beginning without paying for damages.

Jesus came to restore the Holy Spirit in Man.

The mission of Jesus Christ on earth was to reconcile us back to God through the Holy Spirit, by teaching us how to relate, hear, recognise, speak and walk in the Holy Ghost, Furthermore, for there to be a mutual and intimate relationship with the father, Jesus while leaving promised us the Holy Spirit, which is the spirit of the father. This is the medium through which God could reach humanity. Before the ascension of Jesus, the mission of the Holy Spirit was conspicuously stated all across in the scriptures. Some of the activities of the Holy Ghost are:

He teaches, *John 14:26 "But the comforter which is the Holy Ghost, whom the father will send in my name. He shall teach you all things, and brig all things to your remembrance, whatsoever i have said unto you"*

It can be deduced that the Holy Ghost was given to us to teach us. A carnal man cannot understand the word of God for they are foolishness unto him. Therefore, it takes the Holy Spirit to teach us the things of the spirit. Flesh cannot teach spiritual things. The Holy Spirit is also our comforter and constantly reminds us of the word of the father.

Another activity of the Holy Ghost is that, He is the medium of quality and acceptable worship to God. *John4:24 says, "God is a Spirit and they that must worship Him must worship Him in spirit and in truth"*. Anyone without the Holy Spirit cannot offer sacrifice of praise and worship to God. He only accepts our sacrifices, if they are borne out of the spirit. Our prayers and worship will be a mere noise without the presence of the Holy Spirit.

More so, *Romans 8:26 says "Likewise the Spirit also helps our infirmities: for we know not what we should pray as we ought: but the Sprit itself makes intercessions for us with groaning which cannot be altered"*. The best way of praying aright and not amiss is by praying in the Holy Ghost. The Holy Ghost searches the mind of God for us and makes intercessions for us. In other words, the best way of praying the mind of God is by praying in the Spirit.

Additionally, the Holy Spirit is also the spirit of truth. *John16:13 "Howbeit when he, the Spirit of truth, is come, he will guide you into all truth: for he shall not speak of Himself; but whatsoever he shall hear, that shall he speak: and he will show you things to come"*. The Holy Spirit gives the truth, *John 8:32 "And you shall know the truth, and the truth shall make you free"*. *John17:17 Says "Sanctify them through thy truth:*

thy word is truth". When you know the truth in the word of God revealed to you by the Holy Spirit, you become free from every lies of the devil. "Now the Lord is that Spirit: and where the Spirit of the lord is, there is liberty".

Everything a man needs to know about the father is in the Spirit of God. That is, the Holy Ghost is God in us. Little wonder the assignment of Jesus was tailored towards relationship with the Spirit of God.

The ultimate goal of Jesus' assignment on earth was to restore the Holy Spirit in the heart of man, but before this could happen, He had to first re-introduce the kingdom and to restore our righteous and holiness through His blood. Only when we were cleansed and holy once again would we be suitable vessels for the Holy Spirit's indwelling presence.

WHY THE HOLY SPIRIT SO IMPORTANT?

The Holy Spirit is so important because He is the link, the spiritual connection between us and the kingdom of God. He is the one who fills us with spiritual power, guides us, leads us into the knowledge of the truth and brings to our remembrance all the things that Jesus taught. Jesus promised His disciples that after He left He would send the Holy Spirit to be with us forever.[15]

The Holy Spirit could not come until Jesus had completed His work on the cross, risen from the dead and applied His blood for the cleansing of man's sin. Once we were cleansed and made holy again, we were ready to receive the Holy Spirit so that we may reign again. This is confirmed by the scriptures which state "On the evening of that first day of the week, when the disciples were together, with the doors locked for fear of the Jewish leaders, Jesus came and stood among them and said, "Peace be with you!" After he said this, he showed them his hands and side. The disciples were overjoyed when they saw the Lord. Again Jesus said, "Peace be with you! As the Father has sent me, I am sending you." And with that he breathed on them and said, "Receive the Holy Spirit. If you forgive anyone's sins, their sins are forgiven; if you do not forgive them, they are not forgiven." (John 20:19-23) (NIV)

---

[15] But the Advocate, the Holy Spirit, whom the Father will send in my name, will teach you all things and will remind you of everything I have said to you. (John 14:26) (NIV)

In the evening of the very day of the week He rose from the dead, Jesus appeared to His disciples, breathed on them, and imparted the Holy Spirit to them. Later, on the day Pentecost, they would receive the infilling of the Holy Spirit in power, but here Jesus released the Holy Spirit to them as a continuing indwelling presence. By this act, Jesus returned to mankind in the same manner that Adam and Eve had lost in the Garden of Eden. The connection was restored. All who would believe and trust Jesus Christ for the forgiveness of their sins and commit their lives to Him would receive the Holy Spirit. Therefore, regain their connection and citizenship in the kingdom of God. They could then know the will of God, and through them, His will could be done on the earth.

Religion versus Relationships

"Jesus came to restore a kingdom to mankind through relationship and not religion"

What is a Religion?

According to Oxford Dictionary, A Religion is, "the belief in and worship of a superhuman controlling power, especially a personal God or gods."

In that respect, Christianity can be classified as a religion. However, practically speaking Christianity has a key difference that separates it from other belief systems that are considered religion. That difference is RELATIONSHIP.

Most religion, theistic or otherwise, is man-cantered. Any relationship with God is based on man's hard works. A theistic religion, such as Judaism or Islam holds to the belief in a supreme God or gods. While, non-theistic religions such as Buddhism and Hinduism focuses on metaphysical thought patterns and spiritual "energies.", but most religions are similar in that they are built upon the concept that man can reach a higher power or state of being through his own efforts, which is impossible. But surprisingly in most religions, man is the aggressor and the deity is the beneficiary of man's efforts, sacrifices, or good deeds. Paradise, nirvana or some higher state of being is man's reward for his strict adherence to whatever system of belief that religion prescribes.

In that regard, Christianity is not a religion; it is a relationship that God has established with His children. In Christianity, God is the aggressor and man is the beneficiary *(Romans 8:3 "For what the law could not do, in that it was weak through the flesh, God sending His own son in the likeness of sinful flesh, and for sin, condemned sin in the flesh")(KJV).*[16] The Bible states clearly that there is nothing man can do to make himself right with God *(Isaiah 53:6 " All we like sheep have gone astray; we have turned everyone to his own way; and the LORD had laid on him the iniquity of all"(KJV);Isaiah 64:6; "But we are all as unclean thing, and all our righteousness are as filthy rags; and we all do fade as a leaf; and our iniquities like the wind has taken us away(KJV)"Romans 3:23; "For all have sinned and have come short the glory of God(KJV)"Romans 6:23 "For the wages of sin is death; but the gift of God is eternal life through Jesus Christ our lord" KJV).*[17] According to Christianity, God did for us what we cannot do

---

[16] Romans 8:3 For what the law could not do, in that it was weak through the flesh, God sending his own Son in the likeness of sinful flesh, and for sin, condemned sin in the flesh:

[17] Isaiah 53:6 All we like sheep have gone astray; we have turned–every one–to his own way; and the LORD has laid on him the iniquity of us all. (53:6; ESV)

Isaiah 64: 6 - But we are all as an unclean thing, and all our righteousness are as filthy rags; and we all do fade as a leaf; and our iniquities, like the wind, have taken us away.

Romans 3:23 For all have sinned, and come short of the glory of God;

Romans 6:23 For the wages of sin is death; but the gift of God is eternal life through Jesus Christ our Lord.

for ourselves *(Colossians 2:13; "And you, being dead in your sins and in the uncircumcision of your flesh, hath he quickened together with him, having forgiven you all trespasses"(KJV) 2 Corinthians 5:21 "For He hath made him to be sin for us, who knew no sin; that he might be made the righteousness of God in him"(KJV))*. Our sin separates us from His presence, and sin must be punished (Romans 6:23; Matthew 10:28; 23:33). But, because God loves us, He took our punishment upon Himself. All we must do is accept God's gift of salvation through faith (Ephesians 2:8–9; 2 Corinthians 5:21). Grace is God's blessing on the undeserving.

The relationship between God and man is the foundation of Christianity and the antithesis of religion. Established religion was one of the committed enemies of Jesus Christ during His earthly ministry. When God gave His Law to the Israelites, His desire was that they "love the Lord your God with all your heart and with all your soul and with all your strength" (Deuteronomy 6:5; Matthew 22:37). "Love" speaks of relationship. Obedience to all the other commands had to stem from a love for God. We are able to love Him "because He first loved us" (1 John

4:19). However, by Jesus' time, the Jewish leaders had made a religion out of God's desire to live in a love relationship with them (1 Timothy 1:8; Romans 7:12). Over the years, they had perverted God's Law into a works-based religion that alienated people from Him (Matthew 23:13–15; Luke 11:42).

Then they added many of their own rules to make it even more burdensome to people (Isaiah 29:13; Matthew 15:9). They prided themselves on their ability to keep the Law at least outwardly and weighed down their authority over the common people who could never keep such exhausting rules. The Pharisees, as expert as they were at rules keeping, failed to recognise God Himself when He was standing right in front of them (John 8:19). They had chosen religion over relationship.

Just as the Jewish leaders made a religion out of a relationship with God, many people do the same with Christianity. Entire denominations have followed the way of the Pharisees in creating rules not found in Scripture. Some who profess to follow Christ are actually following man-made religion in the name of Jesus. While claiming to believe Scripture, they are often plagued with fear and doubt that they may not be good enough to earn salvation or that God will not accept them if they don't perform to a certain standard. This is religion masquerading as Christianity, and it is one of Satan's favourite tricks. Jesus addressed this in Matthew 23:1–7 when He rebuked the Pharisees. Instead of pointing people to heaven, these religious leaders were keeping people out of the kingdom of God.

CHAPTER 7

THE KINGDOM IS NOT A RELIGION BUT A RELATIONSHIP

The kingdom is not a religion because religion is man's search for God. With the kingdom, the search is over because God has revealed himself to man and sent His son to set us free from our sin and restore us to himself. The kingdom is not a religion but a relationship with the living Christ through faith in His redemption.

Religion is slightly different from relationship in that:

Religion says this is where to worship God, and relationship says you can worship God anywhere. The venue for the worship of God in truth and in spirit is no longer in a temple outside there but in a temple inside us. The Bible says we are the temple of God. The Pharisees and Sadducees exhibited religion, while Jesus came to show us relationship. Religion encourages us to give our tithes and offerings but in relationship you give God your best and all. Jesus told the rich man, of course you pay your tithe and offering, its fine but may I ask you one more thing. Jesus said sell all that you have and give to the poor but he couldn't. That's another glaring difference between religion and relationship. Religion is static while relationship is dynamic. God is the same always but of course you can see Him in various dimensions. Religion makes you attend church services very well but it is relationship that urges and makes you have a personal altar in your secret place. These are few of the differences, which you would agree that the righteousness of man needs to supersede that of the Pharisee.

Of all the faith systems in the world right now, the kingdom alone is effective because it alone has the blood of Jesus Christ, which takes away the sin of man. It alone has the Spirit of God dwelling in the lives of believers. It alone can restore us to righteousness and holiness. Holiness and obedience to the Scripture are important; they are signs of a transformed heart, not a means to attain it. God desires that we be holy as He is holy (1 Peter 1:16). He wants us to grow in grace and knowledge of Him (2 Peter 3:18). But we do these things because we are His children and want to be like Him, not in order to earn His love as religious people.

CHAPTER 8

THE BLOOD OF JESUS CHRIST

The blood of Jesus Christ is key. No matter how often we go to church, no matter how active we are, no matter how many times we receive communion, no matter how much money we give in the offering, and no matter how much time we spend helping the poor or the sick, unless we confessed Jesus Christ as our saviour and Lord and allowed His blood to cover and cleanse us, we are nothing but lost sheep and aliens from the kingdom of God. Good works will not cut it. Sound theology will not fix it. Correct doctrine will not solve it, but only the blood of Jesus Christ can cleanse us of sin and make us righteous and holy again. Good works, sound theology and correct doctrine are the by-products of a growing life in the Spirit. But apart from the blood of Jesus, they have no power. Salvation is not something a person can fake, its either you are saved or not. That you were born into a Christian home doesn't guarantee you an automatic salvation. Except you have a personal encounter with Christ and His cleansing blood, you are far from it. Do you know that; the fact that you handle sensitive and prestigious title or office in church doesn't make you saved. Salvation is not something we should be confused about; can a grown up forget is name? No! So is it for salvation, you must be intentional, deliberate and certain about it

Jesus came to reintroduce the kingdom of God to mankind and restore us to righteousness and holiness. He accomplished this by dying on the cross, where His shed blood had the power to cover and wash away our sin. As a result of our sin we were spiritually dead, slaves to our sin and captive to Satan and his kingdom of darkness. By his death on the cross, Jesus paid the ransom to free us from Satan's grip. He became our substitute so that we could go free.

Jesus became sin for us so that we could

become the righteousness of God through faith in Him alone (2 Corinthians 5:21). His dead body lay in the tomb for three days, lifeless. Death could not hold him. On the morning of that third day, He rose from the dead. Jesus resurrection guarantees that all who have been washed clean of sin by His blood will also share in His life, which is eternal life.

CHAPTER 9

RETURNING HOME

It delights God to see His children come back to Him and it is the pleasure of God that all men come to repentance and be saved. The extent of your sinfulness is not what matters at this time, how deep you have gone in atrocities is not what we need now, the horrible dimensions of immoral deeds does not count here now. What counts is your salvation. What counts is your genuine repentance, and what matters here is your new relationship with the father. God doesn't detest a sinner but of a surely He hates sin.

Severally in this book, we highlighted the benefits and activities of the Holy Spirit. And I am sure you will not want to miss-out in the relationship and fellowship

There is a call from the father for you today. *Matthew 11:28-30 "28. Come unto me, all ye that labour and are heavy laden, and I will give you rest 29. Take my yoke upon you, and learn of me, for I am meek and lowly in heart: and ye shall find rest unto your souls. 30. For my yoke is easy, and my burden is light" (KJV).* Jesus is saying come unto me. Forget about your past, just come to me. Forget about your cruel personality and being notorious, the father is saying just come. He says come unto me all ye that labour and heavy laden. No matter what you are passing through, a call is coming to you today saying come unto me. The only place you can rest is in Christ Jesus, there is no other place where peace and rest can be found. Don't be discouraged by the measure of your hardship or the cumbersomeness of your problems all around you; Just come to Him and He will see you through. *Revelations 3:20 "Behold, I stand at the door, and knock: if any man hears my voice and opens the door, I will come in to him and I will sup with him, and he with me" (KJV).* It is God's joy that a soul is saved into the kingdom.

With respect to the parable of the prodigal son

in Luke 15:11-32, There is an express illustration of a son returning home. What are the things the prodigal son did in relation to making his coming home realistic?

Luke 15:12-13 "12. And the younger of them said unto his father, Father, give me the goods that fall to me, and he divided unto them his living. 13. and not many days after the younger son gathered altogether, and took is journey unto a very far country, and there wasted his substance with riotous living" (King James Version).

From the above scripture, it can be seen that the prodigal son made an urgent request and pester his father for speedy response. Several persons are in this situation, whereby they make a request to God and after God answered them, they go far away from Him, they forget Him, they neglect the initial relationship with the father. They believe this singular answer from God is enough for their life time, and no need staying with God. When many people are in tight corners and severe situations, they acknowledge God, they are always constant in service to God but as soon as they get their answers they depart and see no need abiding with God, since what brought them to God has been solved; what then should they stay doing. Just a token of blessing, riches, financial outburst, career stability, marital settlement has made many deserted God. This is where we miss out; most times we come to God because of what we want, and not because of who He is. Hence, many retrogress in their walk with God. The prodigal son went far from his country to avoid monitoring, supervision, disturbance or possibly persuasions to come home. Have you gone far from God because of comfort or whatever it is, there is a call from the father saying return home.

Furthermore, *Luke 14-16. "14. and when he had spent all that he had, there arose a mighty famine in the land; and he began to be in want. 15. And he went and joined himself to a citizen of that country; and he sent him into his field to feed swine. 16. And he would fain have filled his belly with the husks that the swine did eat; and no man gave unto him" (KJV).*

Just like the prodigal son, are you in a state where all you have is no more, are you in a situation that is humiliating and contrary to what you used to be, are you now engaging in serious labour but little result, here is a call for you, come home! The prodigal son exhausted all he had through extravagant life style; he wasted the resources received from his father in a jiffy. He was never productive with it. The substance he had did not increase; instead it decreased till there was nothing more left. When a man leaves his source, he won't get the necessary resources. There is always an environment where something or someone flourishes. If you want to kill fish cheaply and watch it die, just bring it out of the environment (water). Environment is very germane in the productivity of anything. For the first time, the prodigal son had nothing more on him to live on, absolutely nothing. He was in serious want, hence, he went to labour before he could eat, unlike before when everything is freely at his disposal with ease. He resolved to eating the feed of swine, which has never happened before when he was with his father; He became so low and retched. The scripture says "he had no man to help him", the question remains, where were the men who dined and wined with him in the days of plenty; they were all gone. Have you gotten to a stage in your life where no man seems to help you, where no one identifies with you again as friends, it's an indication for you to return home. There is a call saying, come home.

According to *Luke 15:17-18*, *"17, And he came to himself, he said, how many hired servants of my father have bread enough and to spare, and I perish with hunger! 18. And I will arise and go to my father and will say unto him, father I have sinned against heaven and before thee" (KJV)*.

The bible says "And he came to himself". Don't deceive yourself, you know it pretty well that you can't help yourself out of this mess and situation. You know it for sure that you are far from God and you need help from God. Come back home. The prodigal son came to his senses by doing a critical evaluation between him and his father's slaves and he could see that even his father's slaves were far better than him at the moment. He therefore concluded on taking a swift decision, "I will arise". Dear reader, if you are in this state, I beseech you to make this decision too that "I will arise". Arise from that pit of easily besetting sin, arise from those evil companies, arise from your past, and arise from your wretched state. Arise and come home to our father. For how long will you continue to suffer,

161

for how long will you continue to complain, for how long will you continue to weep in secret, for how long will you continue to rise and fall into temptation, for how long will you be under the bondage of addiction. This is the time for you to make the decision of "I will arise". The latter part of the scripture says "I have sinned against heaven and before thee". He acknowledged that he was a sinner, he kept pride away from the scene, and He was so sober and repentant in gesture. He was desperate for a new life and experience. He wasn't coming to render excuse, he realised his shortcomings and he pleaded for mercy. 2chronicles 7:14 "If my people which are called by my name, shall humble themselves, seek my face, pray and turn from their wicked ways then will hear from heaven, forgive their sins and will heal their land". (KJV)

In addition, he didn't just make a decision but acted promptly on his decision. Many have stayed at the junction of decision for years. All they had been saying is "I will", "I shall", but will not do them. The decision to come to the father is not something to debate that long. *Luke 15:20&22, "20.And he arose and came to his father. But when it was yet a far way off, his father saw him and had compassion, and ran and fell on his neck and kissed him." 22. But the father said to his servants, bring forth the best robe, and put it on him; a ring on his hand and shoes on his feet".* (KJV)

Even when he was a far way off, his father ran towards him, embraced him and held a big feast for him. The father killed the fattest calf, and put on him the best robe. Nothing was mentioned concerning his past again. Who told you that your sin is to too heavy for God to forgive you, why do you think you are too bad for God to embrace, it is a lie of the devil to think that God has forgotten you and abandoned you. God is looking for a repentant heart and humble mind. I don't care how far and how deep you have gone with the devil. There is an assurance that if you make this decision like the prodigal son, the father will accept you heartily and generously. The father didn't give him a substandard welcome neither did he treat him abruptly but with the fullness of joy, he embraced him. The prodigal son told the father to make him one of the slaves but the father treated him otherwise. Ephesians 3:20 "Now unto him that is able to do exceeding abundantly above all that we ask or think, according to the power that works in us". Hannah said if God can just give me a male child. She asked for a male child but gave him additional five children. Solomon asked for wisdom and God gave him riches with it, Hagar the maid of Abraham was given a bottle of water but God gave her a well in the desert. This God is able to do above what you can ever think of. Return home, return to your father, return to your manufacturer, return to you source and return to His presence.

"The Father desires you to come home now"

I believe you; yes, you, who are reading this book right now, you are at the right place at the right moment. You have an opportunity to receive your dominion rulership authority over the earth again through a relationship with the one who legally gave it to you from the beginning. By accepting and confessing Jesus Christ as your Lord and personal saviour through faith, you will then instantly receive the reconnection of the Holy Spirit back in your life right there where you are now to be called a Son of God again. (John 1:12, 13). Yet to all who did receive him, to those who believed in his name, he gave the right to become children of God, children born not of natural descent, nor of human decision or a husband's will, but born of God.

I therefore challenge you to embrace and accept the invitation of the King, Jesus Christ, to come and renew your citizenship in the kingdom of heaven by being born into the kingdom of God through the reception of the Holy Spirit, by accepting the provision of the redemptive work of the King Himself. This is your opportunity, not to join a religion or become a slave of rituals or traditions that have no practical meaning, but rather to migrate from the kingdom of darkness to the kingdom of light and renew your heavenly immigration status on earth.

The kingdom is not about signing up for a religion. The kingdom of God is about being born into the family of God (John 3:3). It is a relationship. Just as an adopted child has no power to create an adoption, we have no power to join the family of God by our own efforts. We can only accept His invitation to know Him as Father through adoption (Ephesians 1:5; Romans 8:15). When we join His family through faith in the death and resurrection of Jesus, the Holy Spirit comes to live inside our hearts and gives us our dominion rulership authority over the earth again as God intended from the beginning of creation (1 Corinthians 6:19; Luke 11:13; 2 Corinthians 1:21–22). He then empowers us to live like children of the King. He does not ask us to try to attain holiness by our own strength, as religion does. He asks that our old self be crucified with Him so that His power can live and be demonstrated through us (Galatians 2:20; Romans 6:6). God wants us to know Him, to draw near to Him, to pray to Him, and love Him above everything. That is not religion; that is a relationship.

CHAPTER 10

MY PRAYER

My ultimate prayer is that you may rediscover your true identity through rediscovering your place in the kingdom of God as His representative king ruler over this planet called earth. You were born to be born-again. It is your choice and your destiny. Welcome home to your dominion ruler-ship authority, and acknowledges Him truly as King of the kings and Lord of the lords.

Glossary

➢HUMANS – Dust of the ground

➢MAN – spirit- came out of God Himself.

RE-DISCOVERY PERSONAL PROFILE

THERE IS ABSOLUTELY NOTHING IN THIS WORLD MORE FRUSTRATING THAN NOT KNOWING OR UNDERSTAND YOUR IDENTITY, WHO YOU TRULY ARE AND THE PURPOSE OF YOUR LIFE. I TRULY BELIEVE THAT WHETHER WE LIKE IT OR NOT, THIS QUESTION OF PURPOSE TENDS TO HAVE POWER OVER EVERYTHING THAT SURROUNDS OUR DAILY LIVES AS IT CONSTRUCTS US TO ACT AND BEHAVE ACCORDINGLY. WHEN WE HAVE NO CLEAR IDEA OF WHO WE TRULY ARE, WE BASE WHO WE SHOULD BE ON THE IMAGE THAT SOCIETY PRESENTS TO US.

CONSEQUENTLY, WE LIVE OUR LIVES BEHIND THE IDENTITY OF OTHER PEOPLE, IMITATING THEIR IDENTITY, RATHER THAN SPENDING THE TIME TO RE-DISCOVER WHO WE REALLY ARE.

HENCE WHY I HAVE TAKING THE TIME TO PUT THIS PROFILE TOGETHER TO HELP YOU RE-DISCOVER, EVALUATE AND RECOGNISE YOUR AUTHORITY, GIFTING AND PERSONAL PURPOSE.

GOD BLESS YOU.

1. WHAT IS MY DEEPEST DESIRE?

(Not what I have a general or passing "interest" in, but rather a deep yearning or aspiration to do.)

2. WHAT AM I TRULY PASSIONATE ABOUT?

(What do I really care about? What gifts and abilities do I especially enjoy using?)

3. WHAT MAKES ME ANGRY?

(Not destructive anger, which is selfishly motivated, but constructive anger that is based on compassion for others and a desire for people to be treated right, anger that is grieved by injustices and that leads to positive action to remedy problems.)

4. WHAT IDEAS ARE PERSISTENT IN MY HEART AND THOUGHTS?

(What recurring dreams do I have for my life?

What idea never leaves me?)

5. WHAT DO I CONSTANTLY IMAGINE MYSELF DOING?

(What do I dream about becoming? What gifts or skills would I use and develop in order to become this?)

6. WHAT DO I WANT TO DO FOR HUMANITY?

(What kind of impact would I like to have on my community? What do I want to pass along to the next generation? What would I like to be remembered for?)

7. WHAT WOULD BRING ME THE GREATEST FULFILLMENT?

(What three endeavors or achievements have given me the greatest satisfaction and fulfillment in life so far, and why? What motivates and gratifies me the most, and how can I incorporate it into my life as my vocation or life focus?)

8. WHAT WOULD I DO FOR NO MONEY OR OTHER COMPENSATION?

(What activities am I currently receiving satisfaction from that I'm not being paid for?

What am I so dedicated to that I would continue to do it even if I stopped receiving money for it? What would I do for no compensation?

9. WHAT WOULD I RATHER BE DOING?

(What do I wish I were doing when I am doing other things? What makes me feel most at home when I am doing it?

10. WHAT WOULD I DO IF I KNEW I COULD NOT FAIL?

(What endeavour, enterprise, creative work, project, or plan would I engage in if it were risk-free? If money were no object? If I didn't worry that I had the wrong background, the wrong looks, the wrong job experiences, or the wrong anything else?)

11. WHAT IS THE MOST IMPORTANT THING I COULD DO WITH MY LIFE?

(Above all other things, what is the most significant thing I could do with my life? What do I want to occur in my life? How do I want to live my life based on my

values and beliefs?)

12. WHAT ENDEAVOR OR ACTIVITY

WOULD BEST CONNECT ME TO MY CREATOR?

(What draws me closest to God?)

SUMMARY STATEMENT:

WHAT I BELIEVE I WAS PUT ON THIS EARTH TO DO:

- *Documenting your personal purpose and gift: In what specific ways have I exercised this gift in the past? How can I build on this in the future?*
- *Exercising and refining your personal gift: In what ways will I develop and apply my personal gift now that I know what it is?*
- *Releasing your personal gift: Who has the knowledge, skills, and commitment to help me to release my gift?*

Contact:

For further information please contact **Claver** on: Facebook: **CLAVER LUKOKI**

Instagram: **CLAVER LUKOKI**

Email: purposeofexistence@hotmail.com

Printed in Great Britain
by Amazon